1999

FirstGroup becomes the second largest operator of yellow school buses in North America with the purchase of Bruce Transportation and Ryder Public Transportation Services

Glasgow Overground bus network introduced

2003

FirstGroup buys Coach USA's transit division, operator of buses in states such as California, Florida and New York

GB Railways, operator of Anglia Rail, GB Rail and Hull Trains bought by FirstGroup

FirstGroup wins Transpennine Express franchise

2005

Greater Western rail franchise won

FirstGroup wins Thameslink Great Northern rail franchise and renames it First Capital Connect

2008

First ScotRail franchise extended to 2014

1998

FirstGroup doubles its size with the acquisition of Great Western Holdings, the operators of Great Western trains

2000

FirstGroup launches the Croydon Tramlink service; the first trams for 50 years in London

2004

FirstGroup wins ScotRail franchise

2007

FirstGroup enters continental Europe with purchase of three German bus companies

2009

Firstgroup's new global headquarters opens in Aberdeen

An incredible journey…

An incredible journey...
the First story

Martin Helm

 GRANTA EDITIONS

© FirstGroup, 2009

Published by Granta Editions, 25–27 High Street, Chesterton, Cambridge CB4 1ND, United Kingdom.
Granta Editions is a wholly owned subsidiary of Book Production Consultants Ltd.

ISBN 978 1 85757 096 0

A CIP catalogue record for this book is available from The British Library.

Picture acknowledgements
All illustrations are from the collections of FirstGroup plc except the following, reproduced with the kind permission of:

Alvey & Towers, pp. 71, 126, 192–3; BridgePhoto.dk, p. 124 (bottom); Bristol International Airport, p. 45; Corbis, pp. 35 (centre and bottom), 41, 113 (left), 186 (top); EpicScotland, pp. 78, 116; flickr.com, pp. 56, 105; gardentrains.co.uk, p. 35 (top); Getty images, pp. 6, 33 (right), 131, 182 (bottom), 187, 188; Dennis Hardley Photography, pp. 52–3, 67, 128–9; Ross Johnston/Newsline Scotland, p. 25; Colin J. Marsden, pp. 34, 57, 59, 61, 64, 65, 73 (left), 125, 162, 190, 191 (left), 194, 195; NetworkRail, pp. 172, 173; Linda Nylind/ Guardian News & Media Ltd 2007, pp. 140–1; Trevor Smallwood, pp. 47, 49.

Front Cover: Jon Arnold/Getty Images.

Every effort has been made to obtain permission for the reproduction of the illustrations and photographs in this book; apologies are offered to anyone whom is has not been possible to contact.

Designed by Peter Dolton.
Design, editorial and production in association with Book Production Consultants Ltd,
25–27 High Street, Chesterton, Cambridge CB4 1ND, United Kingdom.
Printed and bound in Italy by Studio Fasoli, Verona, Italy.

Printed on Symbol Freelife Satin, Fedrigoni Verona FSC - mixed CQ - COC - 000010

Contents

Foreword

This book tells the incredible story of how a local-authority-owned bus company in Aberdeen turned itself into the largest public transport operator in the UK and North America within the space of just twenty years. Today it ranks among the UK's hundred largest companies.

This small company carrying just 96,000 passengers a day in the mid 1980s now carries more passengers in three days than it used to in an entire year, and has a turnover of some £6 billion a year. It has grown from a staff of 600 to a giant employing more than 137,000. Along the way it has introduced innovation, technology, enthusiasm and investment on a scale local transport has not seen before. It has brought a revolutionary focus on delivery – a word sometimes unfamiliar to the public sector whose services it took over.

The one common thread through this story is that the man who led that bus company in Aberdeen in the 1980s – Moir Lockhead – has continued to lead and guide the company throughout and is still Chief Executive today. His achievements for the company and the country were finally recognised in a 2008 knighthood as Sir Moir Lockhead for services to transport.

Though this book was commissioned by FirstGroup, I agreed to write it only if I were given total editorial freedom and allowed to set the company's progress in the context of the political, economic, regulatory, media and motoring climate in which it had to operate. Set against that background, the speed with which First has progressed becomes even more remarkable.

Public transport is a sector that has to cope with prejudice, misunderstanding, over-regulation and a political framework that often takes the line of least resistance. This book sets out how FirstGroup triumphed in this minefield and gave the user a public transport network that could be relied upon.

I have to admit to being an unashamed admirer of the company, and I have been an adviser to them for many years. My background in politics, central government, journalism and the transport industry has, hopefully, allowed me to set the company's progress against the background in which it developed and allowed me a measure of objectivity.

Martin Helm

The old and the new: Albion RG 1173 bus, restored in 1993, alongside one of the current Aberdeen articulated vehicles.

The foundations

In the beginning

The FTSE 100 Index is the most widely quoted and prestigious index for tracking the London stock market. It lists the shares of the top 100 UK companies, and every large company aspires to join it. The household names on it roll off the tongue – Cadbury, Marks & Spencer, Shell, BP and Rolls-Royce for example: companies that began trading generations ago.

At the end of 2007 they were joined by an upstart company that had not even been created when the Index began in 1984. The name is FirstGroup. Its rise has been phenomenal and could not have been foreseen when five local-authority executives sat down to pitch for the privatisation of the local-authority-owned bus company they worked for in Aberdeen in the late 1980s. They met at the bus depot offices in a former infantry barracks in Aberdeen: the home of Grampian Regional Transport, a local bus company with a fleet of 225 buses and a staff of 600.

They eventually had their way and the company was privatised. Its headquarters is still in the revamped infantry barracks, but today it is one of the UK's largest employers, the largest UK public transport operator, the largest public transport operator in North America and a member of the famed FTSE 100.

The old infantry barracks in King Street, Aberdeen, which has been headquarters for the company even before GRT was privatised in the 1980s. Throughout that time Moir Lockhead's office has been on the top floor alongside the turret.

The scale of its operations is so vast that it is almost impossible to take it in. Each working day the company carries some 9 million passengers right across the United States, Canada, the United Kingdom and in Western Europe aboard a fleet of 80,000 buses and coaches and 2,000 railway carriages served by more than 137,000 staff.

Every hour of the day and night across different time zones and continents, up to 375,000 passengers are boarding First's fleet. Today it takes the company just minutes to pick up the number of passengers that the old Aberdeen operation carried in an entire day in the 1980s.

But the story begins well before that crucial 1980s meeting, in the evolution of Aberdeen itself and the development of its transport network. Remotely sited high up on the north-east coast of Scotland on the same latitude as Alaska and Siberia, Aberdeen looks eastwards over the grey and hostile North Sea. To the west lie the rugged Highlands of Scotland. Aberdeen is known as the Granite City because of the stone of which many of its buildings are made. The city is so far north that in winter daylight hours are few, while in summer it hardly gets dark.

The city began life as a fishing settlement 1,300 years ago. Four centuries on it had become a town and busy port exporting salted fish, hides and wool. By 1495 the city already had its university, one of the earliest in the UK, and it was joined by a second less than a century later. Real growth, though, came in the

One of Aberdeen's early electrified trams in service in 1918.

RIGHT: An early horse-drawn tram. They first came into service in the 1870s.

early nineteenth century when many new buildings – such as St Andrew's Cathedral and the music hall – were put up and amenities improved. The city also gained gas street lighting (to replace whale-oil lamps), filtered water pumped from the river into public wells and a network of sewers.

Then, in 1833, Aberdeen gained its first regular bus services to operate on a fixed route, using an experimental steam bus – the experiment ended when the boiler exploded. So it was back to horse-drawn buses when two new services – Royal Hotel to Stoneywood and King Street to the new railway station – were introduced in 1850. A more lasting network of horse-drawn buses was introduced to the city by William Bain in 1862 when he formed a private company for the purpose. Just twelve years later horse trams supplanted other operations. By 1898 Aberdeen Corporation had bought the tramways and extended the network.

Motor-bus services were trialled in the city at the start of the next century but did not last. Later the First World War gave women the chance to join the tram network: first as 'conductorettes' in 1915, and as drivers in 1917. After the Second World War Aberdeen joined the rest of the UK by abandoning trams in 1955 and starting bus-only operations. In 1975 the council bus services were renamed Grampian Regional Transport (GRT) as a result of local government reorganisation. And so it stayed until two key developments almost coincided.

First, the then Prime Minister Margaret Thatcher aimed to create a competitive market in public transport with the privatisation of local bus services, spelt out in a 1984 White Paper. She wanted local authorities to sell off their bus companies and to allow private-sector operators into the market to compete with them. The Transport Act of 1985 gave the government and local authorities the powers to deliver that change. The same year Moir Lockhead (now Sir Moir), formerly Chief Engineer at Strathclyde Buses in Glasgow, was appointed to his first management job, as general manager, and had to face the prospect

The Canal Road depot and bus fleet between the two world wars, *c.*1927.

The heyday of the bus and tram: the turning point, Castlegate, Aberdeen, in the early 1950s, when roads were traffic free, passenger numbers were at their highest and vehicles were always able to run to time.

Aberdeen 1955 : a view from the
Salvation Army Citadel above
Castlegate, Aberdeen.

of private-sector competition while he was still operating under the constraints of the public sector.

Under the terms of the new 1985 Transport Act local authorities had to set up their municipal bus companies as separate stand-alone companies, albeit still council owned, in preparation for a deregulation of the bus market which would allow private operators to come in and register new routes in competition with council-run services. The whole process was designed to shake up local transport, encourage a choice of services for the consumer and force councils to privatise their own bus services.

GRT was sitting in the middle of this and the options the new directors faced were stark. Lockhead and his fellow directors Robbie Duncan (Finance), Gordon Mills (Engineering), Colin Smith (Operations) and Joe Mackie (Commercial) sat down to look at the choice. Duncan later reported that some of the men around the table were cautious. They could continue to manage the business, watching new private-sector competitor operators nibble away at the profitable bits of it and risking having the company being bought from under them, or they could put together their own bid and borrow the money to buy the company.

'We thought it would be great to have the business but would not have had the audacity on our own,' recalled Duncan. 'It took Moir's leadership. He was one of the guys with the vision and who could make it happen.'

The decision to seek an employee/management buyout became almost inevitable for Lockhead and his management team. They had already worked with the local authority to set up the municipal operation as a stand-alone business with the council as its single shareholder. The big difference for the management team was that until that moment bus managers had been responsible purely for operations. Policy and accounting were down to local councils.

Just eight months after GRT became a stand-alone company Lockhead and the team faced the moment of truth on 26 October 1986 – Deregulation Day. From that day all Grampian's routes were exposed to competition from other operators, notably the Scottish Bus Group (SBG) through its subsidiary Northern Scottish. And in they came, cherry picking the routes where they thought they could make most money and cause most damage.

Lockhead recalls those days well: 'Of course, the incumbent had an advantage if he was running the services well since he had the strength of a network behind him.'

GRT left nothing to chance. Northern Scottish's manager, Lockhead's predecessor at Aberdeen, had warned them he would be competing against them just a few days before registration of routes closed. 'In a game of poker our guys were smarter and were aggressive against a manager who had left them to go across to SBG. We even had a competition to see who could best guess which of our routes they would register.' A defence strategy was put in place.

But defence was not the only strategy. GRT registered services of its own in Northern Scottish territory. Neither side made money in opposition territory and a year later SBG pulled back, allowing GRT to regroup. For the moment the threat had been seen off.

However Lockhead, the managers, unions and staff had all watched with horror what was happening to the former public-sector bus companies in England, particularly the old National Bus Company. 'Assets were being stripped out, pensions closed down. Bad practices were emerging. This was not yet happening in Scotland but there was a general feeling it was inevitable,' said Lockhead. 'Our staff, through the trade unions, asked what we could do to avoid that, becoming victims of the process.'

A buyout looked the obvious choice. But, while it might make good business sense to managers and staff, it made precious little sense to the company's owners, Grampian Regional Council. Under Lockhead services were running smoothly, operations were now making a profit and the business was no longer a drain on either council management time or resources.

The management was advised that if they took a proposal to the council too early and the answer was no, they would never get agreement later on. Crunch time came in 1988 when the Scottish Secretary announced the privatisation of SBG.

'The founder member of the GRT board, the late Councillor Jack Dempsey, told us: "That's your trigger. You are now under threat,"' explained Lockhead. 'He said "If you wait, the rules will be made for you, but no one has done it in Scotland yet."'

This was a sale that was going to take a lot of diplomacy, a great deal of politicking and the co-operation of trade unions and staff. All needed to be persuaded that this was a deal that was good for the taxpayer, the voter, the council, the community, the bus user and the staff.

The council and unions were keen that the buyout should be employee led, so the management team and the company's lawyer Sid Barrie (now First's commercial director), a partner at Paull & Williamsons, and accountant David Shearer, a Touche Ross partner, concocted a winning formula. Management would own 51 per cent of the new company, employees 33 per cent and two locally based financial institutions 16 per cent. The staff would all be given shares, the number depending on their number of years' service at the depot. In addition the staff would get two employee directors, chosen by them, on the board to ensure their interests were protected.

In return the new company would pay the council £5 million to take the

Restored Albion bus No. RG1173 turning into King Street, Aberdeen.

225 vehicles, 600 staff and 2 depots (in Aberdeen and Dyce) off their hands. The bid represented the net asset value of the business. The council saw the staff were well protected, their main concern, and the proposal went to Scottish Secretary Malcolm Rifkind with their blessing.

As the day for privatisation approached the strain started to tell on the management team. None had been a company director until two years earlier – and then only of a council-owned company. Suddenly they were going to be on their own, with big debts and responsibilities to investors and staff. Outside the sharks circled ready to pick off a business if it looked vulnerable. As crunch day came for the managers to sign up to their stake in the business with its incumbent responsibilities, one wavered and said he could not do it that day. Lockhead told him that if he could not, his shares would have to be divided up among the others. After a hurried telephone conversation with his wife, the waverer decided to sign. It must have been one of the best decisions he ever made.

Finally, Malcolm Rifkind gave the government go-ahead and GRT was set free to fend for itself. After agreeing to pay a further £500,000 as a premium on the net asset value, the privatised GRT was launched onto the world. None of the directors, let alone the staff, had a clue what lay in store for the future.

Lockhead recalled: 'We had a few moments of fear of the unknown. We were out in the wide world. We had shareholders to deal with, a business to run and no one standing behind us.'

Throughout the process Lockhead had picked the brains of his advisers. One had warned him, 'It's all about the cash' – something that has always stuck with him. An otherwise successful business could easily go under if it

A 1958 AEC Regent V MD2RA bus travelling over the Bridge of Don, Aberdeen.

did not keep its cash flow under control. Lockhead never forgot that, and in the early days he would be seen regularly in the bus depot counting room as drivers brought the fares boxes back in so he could understand the impact of heavy traffic, weather or fare changes on cash flow.

A common memory of those early days was one of belt tightening. The company had to make better margins to service its borrowings and shareholders, to make itself more efficient and to grow the revenue. That meant, they remembered, that investment would have to wait. However the new company's first annual report makes clear that, even then, investment was by no means choked off. It had spent over £1 million on new property (£260k) and fleet replacement (£770k), while putting £1.7 million into reserves and not declaring a dividend.

The innovation, investment and introduction of new technology which is today the hallmark of First's operations were also part of the bedrock on which the company developed, as early company reports demonstrated. At the outset the company recorded that, following a fleet-wide trial, GRT had 'continued its use of the farecard system which eliminated the requirement for passengers to carry cash by means of a pre-encoded magnetic card ticket'.

The report for 1989 recorded: 'The buyout did create short term financial pressures and we had to produce increased profits to cover the repayment of

Delivery of a fleet of 1959 AEC Regent V MD2RA buses.

the loan. Despite this the company produced its best trading results on record and created the confidence to allow further growth through the acquisition of Kirkpatrick of Deeside in June.'

From the outset it was GRT's practice to involve their staff: 'We continued our investment in training and development with the introduction of team briefing. We were able to offer a more regular communications system and this was followed by a series of customer care training days which were attended by over 600 of our employees from all sections of the company.' It paid off, as the newly privatised company was soon able to record: 'It was rewarding to see and hear the strength of commitment and enthusiasm from all staff and the link between behaviour within the individual staff groups and the quality of service we provide was clearly established.'

The attention to promotion and market research was later acknowledged when the company was awarded the 1991 Scottish Marketing Award in the corporate sector. Judges' comments related to work that had been done on customer care, the marketing of bus services through 'Just the ticket' and the development of the farecard system, in addition to the move from local services into long-distance and continental work.

'This was all about survival,' said Lockhead. 'We had a lot to do to make us stronger. We had to make higher margins and we were able to set targets based on the staff getting more shares.'

And, as Joe Mackie, one of the original managers – who remains at the Aberdeen bus company as commercial director – explained, their shares certainly did well. Of the six hundred workers in the original company, Mackie reckons that some long-serving staff eventually probably made £100,000 from their free shares. Certainly Robbie Duncan, who was to become Lockhead's right-hand man for the next fifteen years and was at the heart of the later successes, recalls that quite a few of the senior drivers would have made that amount – 'a lot of money for someone earning £13,000 a year'.

But before anyone was able to cash in, there was lots to do. Costs had to be driven down, performance improved, investments made and the public encouraged to use buses more. Not all staff survived. While there was a continuing need for all the drivers, the back office was staffed to normal public-sector levels and needed to be cut back to the levels usually seen in commercial businesses.

Share ownership though brought out the best in staff. As Alec Bodie, a driver for twenty-six years, told the local paper, the *Aberdeen Press & Journal*: 'I see

Daimler bus travelling along Aberdeen's Union Street in the late 1960s.

my future and that of my own company as being in my own hands now. It's up to us to ensure the customers get the type of service they need.'

Evan Watt, another driver, reinforced that: 'The public will certainly benefit from the added commitment that comes from the staff being the new owners of the company. It's more than just a job now which is far more satisfying for us all.'

Soon afterwards, another local newspaper, the *Evening Express*, reported a practical demonstration of the new attitude. They told the story of how a company driver had looked after the group when a teacher became ill on a school trip to Paris. The school 'wrote to us later and were particularly pleased at how he had handled it,' the company told the paper.

But the earlier worries about the risks of going into the private sector were confirmed by the pre-privatisation Chairman, the late Mr John Fotheringham, who joined the board in December 1987 and reported a year later that:

> *The difficulties facing a local-authority department with the commercial realities of a deregulated environment must have offered a daunting prospect in those early days. I was pleased to find there had been such a willing acceptance of the changed environment by the whole workforce and that the new competitive operating conditions had whetted the appetite for further development.*

Looking back at GRT's early annual reports, the tell-tale signs of its future success were there from the outset. For a young company and a management team with no experience of the private sector, the maturity of their decisions was incredible. Part of that was down to one of the founder non-executive directors who has been on the board from day one and is now the company Chairman, Martin Gilbert. He is a founder shareholder of Aberdeen Asset Management, where he is Chief Executive, and his company bought an 8 per cent stake in GRT when it was privatised.

From the first annual report GRT was demonstrating the need to control costs, to hit targets, to carry their workforce with them, to invest in passenger growth, to work with their stakeholders and to market the products to achieve more growth. Today that might not seem incredible, but this was an industry not known for trying – let alone achieving – a single one of these objectives. What was also remarkable was that these early developments flew in the face of so many of the developments happening in England at the time.

Deregulation generally was giving bus operations a bad name – one that went on to sour the views of passengers, politicians and pundits alike for a generation. Bus wars had broken out with niche operators trying to cherry pick the most profitable routes. The most smoky, garishly coloured old bangers were chasing each other down the roads, clogging high streets and angering the passengers who just wanted a regular, reliable bus service.

Pirate buses would be positioned to run just ahead of traditional scheduled services so they could cream off all the passengers. Meanwhile some bus operations in the public sector were put under siege. Private-sector pirates ran free services in competition against them to starve them into submission. Some tried to poach entire driving fleets.

So just what were GRT doing differently and why? Time and place had something to do with it, but so did the nature of the buyout and its Managing Director. As for time and place, the privatisations in England had started earlier and both Aberdeen staff and managers had had a chance to recoil in horror at the slash and burn taking place at once proud bus operations and on seeing the naked – and very unappealing – warfare going on south of the border. No one wanted to see similar savage cuts imposed in Scotland. Being tucked away in the north east of Scotland did no harm either. With such juicy pickings in markets they understood, why would the Sassenachs want to go hunting in

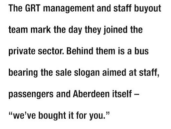

The GRT management and staff buyout team mark the day they joined the private sector. Behind them is a bus bearing the sale slogan aimed at staff, passengers and Aberdeen itself – "we've bought it for you."

markets they could not begin to understand? And then there were Lockhead and the team. Slash and burn was not a concept an engineer with a reputation for building and creating and an attention to detail could relate to.

Public versus private

Looking back, one can easily share the sense of euphoria and freedom that Lockhead, his team and most of the company felt at the time of privatisation. Even though the council's appointees to the board had worked constructively with them, the public-sector ethos and regime stifled innovation, change, growth, customer focus and investment.

Lockhead had not even been allowed to choose his own senior management team. They were selected for him by the council. Robbie Duncan remembers being interviewed by a panel of seven people, one of whom told him to stand up because he could not hear what he was saying sitting down. Investment in new fleet had to join the council queue. Duncan recalls an annual round where, far from producing a business case for investment in new fleet, the company was asked 'Which ten new vehicles would you like this year?'

There was a huge amount of interference in everything from how services would be run, the fares that could be charged and the level of dividend that could be paid. Staff were all on local-authority pay scales and conditions of service – none of which was designed for a private-sector business competing

The changes in two decades		
	GRT 1988	FirstGroup 2008
Turnover	£15 million	£6 billion
Fleet	225 buses and coaches	82,500 buses and coaches 2,000 railway carriages
Staff	600	137,000
Operating area	Aberdeen and Grampian	The entire United States and Canada, across the UK, Germany, Denmark, Sweden and Spain
Passengers carried per year	35 million	3,285 million
Passengers carried per day	96,000	9 million

in the commercial world. Decision-taking went through a long and tortuous approvals process and updating routes and services was not something for the faint hearted.

Shona Byrne, who had joined the company just months before privatisation as a young marketing assistant, remembered how the council focus had been on a business that was operationally efficient, but it did not matter whether the service was needed or what the customer wanted. Robbie Duncan recalled how in some local-authority bus companies the new team would find that, instead of focusing exclusively on maintaining the fleet, some workshops were side-tracked into the rebuilding of old engines, a worthy but hardly commercial role for them.

Privatisation blew all that away at a stroke. Young Shona Byrne recalled the excitement among the staff at the time – not least because everyone had a financial stake in the new business's success. What impressed her most, though, was the new speed of decision-taking and the short chain of command. 'Moir was inspirational and a real person of the people. You would just chat to him in the corridor about an idea and things happened. People were a little nervous but with Moir at the helm they were motivated.'

Lockhead – the driving force

The one common thread throughout the history of FirstGroup has been the company's leader from public-sector ownership through to the transport giant it is today: Moir Lockhead. He has always been the man for all occasions, driving from the front, inspiring, challenging, probing. He stretches everyone to their limits, helps people achieve what they considered to be impossible, and is a strategist who has been mapping out the next steps for the company – plotting several moves ahead. He has pushed the company from remote Scottish beginnings to become one of the UK's largest 100 companies. The scale of his success can be measured by FirstGroup's turnover. It now takes more in fares in under ten hours than it did in a whole year just twenty years ago.

Lockhead is a man who has had his eye as much on the welfare of the company's staff as on the share performance and customer satisfaction. There are many pioneering initiatives he has introduced that are still flagship schemes today – held out as an example to other companies. He is as at ease on the shop floor as he is in the boardroom; he is as smooth as a politician and he is a natural mouthpiece for his company. Yet here was a man who left school at 15 and was an engineer until the age of 40. It was only then that he became a company director for the first time – and even that was in a local-authority-owned company.

So how did it all start? Some people put it down to Lockhead's attention to detail, which he inherited from his parents. He was born in Sedgefield, County Durham – the former constituency of Tony Blair – to parents who both worked in a nearby psychiatric hospital. His father was a painter/decorator and his mother a seamstress.

'My father was fanatical about doing things properly and my mother the same. They never left anything half done,' recalls Lockhead. 'They were always trying to do things a little bit better, a bit differently. My father was a disciplinarian. My brother and I weren't boxed in. He wanted us to go out and enjoy ourselves but within certain limits. He did not want us to let ourselves down.'

Nonetheless, in 1960, at the age of 15, Lockhead left school. 'It was a classic case of enjoying school but enjoying leaving,' he said. What happened next was typical of Lockhead's ability to get stuck into life quickly. He left school on the Friday night; on the Saturday he met the manager of the local main bus workshops, and on the following Monday he started working there as an engineering apprentice.

He was enrolled in night school, where he studied for two nights a week and emerged at 21 with his City & Guilds qualifications and craftsman's skills. In the early years he would take his pay packet straight home to his mother, who would give him some money back to allow him to go out. However, it was not long before the 19-year-old Moir Lockhead had something else to spend his money on. At the bus company workshops he had set eyes on an attractive 16-year-old office girl called Audrey. A year later they were married and their first son Gary was born in 1965.

There can be no doubt that Audrey helped shape Lockhead's attitude to life and enthusiasm for capitalism. 'Audrey is very organised. She does things thoroughly. Once she makes her mind up something happens,' he said proudly. That helped enormously as Lockhead's career took off. He had soon outgrown his job in Darlington. Management had recognised his ability to get things done. He was quickly made a supervisor and took on responsibilities for testing new products and refurbishing vehicles, but there was nothing left to teach him, so he moved on.

A young and confident-looking Moir Lockhead in his early days at Aberdeen.

He joined a Tarmac subsidiary (the long-distance trucking company Econo-freight) as a trainee manager, learning the basics of finance, operational performance and routing before going back to Hartlepool as fleet engineer to run a small bus depot workshop. Lockhead had decided that while he liked his first taste of management, he liked engineering more. The offer of £1,500 a year running an eighty-bus engineering depot in Hartlepool tempted Lockhead and Audrey away from their council house in West Cornforth. Audrey put her foot down and Lockhead found capitalism. With her parents owning their own home, she told Lockhead bluntly: 'We're not renting houses.'

They were soon moving into a brand-new £4,500 three-bedroom home on Hartlepool's Fens Estate in what was to become a pattern in their lives. Audrey would find the homes, run the building projects and take charge of the family, leaving Lockhead to focus fully on his career during the week and bask in the enjoyment of being surrounded by his family at weekends.

After four years in Hartlepool Lockhead had to find a more challenging role, so in 1973 he was off to Newcastle, where the Passenger Transport Executive, the north-east metropolitan transport organisation, needed an engineering manager to look after three hundred buses across two depots at Byker. His talents were quickly recognised and he was promoted to the job of assistant chief engineer, responsible for nearly six hundred buses across Tyne and Wear.

In 1979, at the age of just 34, he reached one of the pinnacles of local-authority engineering as the Chief Engineer of Strathclyde, covering the whole of the Greater Glasgow area and responsible for both an underground network and more than 1,000 buses. He was the youngest engineer in the sector to hold such a key post. At the time the family were not joining in the celebrations. Lockhead recalls driving the family north to the Scottish border and turning round to see 'Everyone was crying – even the budgie.'

Lockhead arrived in Glasgow to find a bus company that was not in good shape and an underground rail network that was closed for a three-year total refurbishment programme. Time was not on his side. The Queen was coming to open the revamped underground network just months later, and Palace aides had warned him that the train she was travelling on 'had' to be working. A cunning plan was hatched. A train was put on a downhill route so the driver only had to let the brakes off for it to run. It worked, and after the royal visit the line was closed again to allow the restoration to finish.

Another 1979 event helped shape Lockhead's future – the election of

Margaret Thatcher as British Prime Minister. The Iron Lady made no secret of her feelings about the public sector and she soon turned her attention to local transport. Local-authority-owned bus companies were to be put on commercial lines, forced to face competition and encouraged to be sold off.

Lockhead could see not just a threat to his job but a time of great uncertainty and upheaval for the sector. The publication of the 1984 Transport White Paper and the legislation the following year made that clear. Several times he toyed with the idea of buying a few buses and setting up for himself, but eventually he saw an opportunity in the new vacancy for a general manager at the council-run Aberdeen bus company. At least as the head of his own organisation he would be better placed to influence the changes that were to come.

Colleagues have said of Lockhead that he has always been quick to learn from those around him and able to factor in the new dimension that they have brought to the table. Robbie Duncan, a chartered accountant, soon found for example that Lockhead could quickly bore through the figures to what he needed to know and identify how they could be best presented to serve him as a management tool. Bankers, city advisers, stockbrokers, lawyers all found their brains being picked and their perspectives factored into his future game plans.

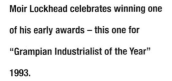

Moir Lockhead celebrates winning one of his early awards – this one for "Grampian Industrialist of the Year" 1993.

Nowadays, with an empire stretching to every corner of the United States, Canada, England, Scotland and Wales and into both Ireland and Germany, much of Lockhead's life is spent at airports or on planes. At each destination there are new challenges, ranging from giving a potential acquisition the once-over to meetings with public-sector customers.

Along the way he will quiz managers about performance, speak at company conferences and carry out a safety tour. Always in the market for new ideas, he can often be found brainstorming with manufacturers, in strategy meetings with fellow directors, seeking opinions from outsiders or briefing major investors. To this day there remains an intense focus on performance, service delivery and the cash. Each month directors face close scrutiny on any perceived service failures, negative customer reaction or dips in revenue. Measures to get delivery back on course are carefully analysed.

Lockhead's skills are sometimes best illustrated through incidents that happened along the way. Some months after the Labour government came to power in 1997, transport ministers organised what they called a 'Bus Summit', getting the industry and local authorities together to set their vision for the industry under the new government. At the last moment John Prescott, then Deputy Prime Minister and Secretary of State for Transport and the Environment, asked Lockhead if he would join him and Gus Macdonald, then Transport Minister, on the top table for a press conference. There was no time to brief him.

Moir Lockhead has grown the company into a successful and expanding empire.

The first question came and Prescott replied to the enquirer 'Err, that one's for you, Gus,' to which the minister responded, 'No, it's over to you, Moir.' Without batting an eyelid or a moment's hesitation Lockhead took on the challenge that both politicians had ducked and came over convincingly while not upsetting the politicians – a difficult task at any time.

One of the finest examples of Lockhead getting the company to achieve the impossible was with the experimental Automatic Train Protection (ATP) braking system on First Great Western's high-speed trains. The system had been trialled by British Rail on the high-speed line between London and Bristol. The in-cab and on-track system will automatically brake a train if it is exceeding the dedicated line speed for that stretch of track – including braking the train if it tries to run a red signal.

British Rail never got it to work reliably – partly to do with the mismatch between 'mature' rolling stock and a sensitive new piece of equipment. At the time of privatisation the system was only working 20 per cent effectively. Engineers had coaxed it up to 80 per cent effectiveness at the time of the Ladbroke Grove railway accident. ATP could not have stopped the accident since it was caused by another train from another company – not fitted with the system – which was able to jump a red light and hit a Great Western train.

Nonetheless Lockhead told the company that in three months' time if ATP was not working on any of his high-speed trains that service would not run. He lambasted the engineers and the manufacturers, who all told him his request was not deliverable. Three months later the system was working – just as it is today some nine years further on. His determination and leadership had triumphed once again.

Lockhead is just not good at being told something 'can't be done' and does not take kindly to people who tell him that. He would much rather someone said to him, 'Yes, we can do it, but this is a better way to do it, it will cost this much and these are the results you will get. Do you still want to go ahead?'

On the other hand, one of the things people repeatedly say they most admire about Lockhead is his willingness to listen to new ideas and then, if he likes them, to back their development. But woe betide anyone who goes to him before they have thought them through. Shona Byrne, the first marketing manager for the company, explained that you could bump into Lockhead in a corridor and pass on your idea, only to have him call you up to his office later in the day to talk about how it would be implemented.

Alistair Darling, who as Transport Secretary launched First's futuristic tram/ bus **ftr** streetcar project, told the launch guests at Greenwich that one of the things he admired about Lockhead and First was the speed with which the company could deliver things. He said that only about a year earlier Lockhead had been to see him to talk about the **ftr** concept, and just twelve months later here he was with the prototype vehicle.

It is not just managers Lockhead listens to, but staff as well. He will some-times run late when he is touring a depot because he has been discussing an issue on the ground with a driver or engineer. If he thinks their points are valid he will go back to the MD of that company and tell him to sort it. Passengers get similar attention. They can be waiting quietly at a bus stop only to find the Chief Executive of the £6 billion-a-year-turnover parent company asking them what they think of the service. They tell him too – he takes note and later in the day raises the issue with the local management.

Managing directors of the bus and rail companies are not always so keen to know that Lockhead is passing through their region. If they did not know all that was going on before, they will quickly find out as a stream of phone calls is received suggesting that some of the buses are not as clean as they should be or some services seem to be bunched up. At First Great Western there were times when managers tried to identify in advance when Lockhead might be using their services. A canny man, he would sometimes change his timetable to catch them by surprise.

Managers at First can find they achieve lightning promotion if they prove they are up for it. Age, sex and background are no barriers to promotion. Delivery is what counts. At one time First had three women managing directors running three of the UK's largest rail franchises. That was unprecedented in an industry that had traditionally been dominated by men. What was important to Lockhead was that they were the best people for the job. He also has an un-canny knack for spotting people who can talk the talk but not walk the walk – both among company staff and advisers. He is not taken in and they do not last long.

For a man who has climbed to the top of the slippery management pole and stayed there for twenty years, creating a business giant, Lockhead shows a lot of understanding of other people. Yet he has never hesitated to be ruthless if he has to be. Senior managers do not let the company down many times before they have to look for another company to work for and yet, even as he is discussing his managers, he is interrupted by his safety director telephoning to say that a child has been run over by a bus. He expresses genuine concern for the child and its family, closely questioning the safety director on how it could have happened before asking about the driver.

Like all good chief executives, he is always ready to listen to outsiders who offer advice on how things could be done better. On the other hand, if it turns out that they actually have little to offer, he will often ask others to let them down gently rather than take the painful action himself.

Chairman Martin Gilbert describes Lockhead as the best operator in the business, although he believes Lockhead can be very cautious over acquisitions (something Lockhead would regard as a virtue rather than a fault). Gilbert remembers Lockhead being very 'value conscious' over the Laidlaw bid and not wanting to pay the extra 25 cents a share the Laidlaw team were after. Only when the Laidlaw team indicated that sum would bring closure did he agree to it.

Sir Moir Lockhead surrounded by his family. Behind Moir, wife Audrey and daughter Claire are (l. to r.) sons Gary, Stuart and Sean.

However hard Lockhead has worked during the week, he tries to keep the weekends for the family. And once the metal gate clangs behind him as he drives onto his 450-acre estate on Royal Deeside, Lockhead will probably remain inside until he goes to work on Monday morning. If he needs to be contacted on his mobile phone at weekends he can sometimes be heard saying proudly that he is sitting on his tractor.

While Lockhead concentrates his energies on the group, Audrey runs the house and garden, and daughter Claire runs the family farm with the same attention to detail that all the family has inherited. Lockhead likes nothing more than to relax around the farm surrounded by his family of three sons, one daughter and eight grandchildren – all of whom live within a radius of twenty miles. Son Gary is a bus driver with the company, Stuart is an oil man and Sean an architect. Lockhead sometimes thinks his children have stayed so close because of the move they made from Tyneside to the very different world of Glasgow and then Aberdeen. They increasingly grew to depend on each other. Lockhead has an obsession with safety and it spills over at home. His grand-children will not ride bikes without helmets and high-visibility jackets.

To this day Lockhead protects his family from the detail of the business. He brought his daughter Claire to the annual company dinner and dance in Aberdeen in 2007 when the Princess Royal was the guest of honour. Claire told First senior corporate managers sitting nearby how surprised she was to hear her father making a speech. 'Is that what he has to do?' she asked them.

Meanwhile at home one of his Highland bulls – nicknamed Jock by the family – had been getting a bit aggressive. Lockhead sent it off early to the abattoir. For the next year Lockhead joked at family barbecues that they were all eating 'Jockburgers'. Squirrels on his estate have better luck. Two varieties of red squirrel are trying to ward off the marauding grey squirrels which dom-inate most of the UK. Lockhead has, typically, given them a helping hand, im-porting vast quantities of cob nuts from Oregon and putting them in special feeders which the smaller red squirrels can use but which tip out the heavier grey animals.

Lockhead is a physically imposing – but gentle – man who smiles often and impresses most people he meets. He is a man who is passionate about his in-dustry and his company. Outside it, he is enthusiastic about rugby and foot-ball, taking his sons with him to watch crucial international matches.

He takes his farming seriously too, and is immensely proud of the fact that

The Princess Royal, the active patron of the Chartered Institute of Transport and Logistics smiles at a Lockhead joke. Moir was receiving the Entrepreneur of the Year Award at the Scottish Business Achievement Award Trust in Edinburgh in 2006.

Moir and his other love, Lily-Anne – one of his treasured Highland cattle.

his Aberdeen Angus beef has been stocked by Marks & Spencer. Like many cattle farmers he has little time for sheep. Once when trying out a company train simulator his instructor pointed out to him that he had just run over a flock of sheep that had strayed onto the line. Lockhead replied: 'That's all right. I'm a cattle man.' Like farmers the world over, he grumbles about the price beef fetches at market, and when lunching with a *Financial Times* journalist in a Marylebone restaurant he remarked that the steak he was eating cost as much as a whole steer of his fetched at market.

Lockhead has a total empathy with the man on the shop floor and what life is like for him – not surprisingly, given that he was once there himself. Having worked his own way up, he has consistently tried to make sure that others across the company have the chance to do the same – whether by offering them the training to reach their personal ceiling or a financial share in the company's success. For those who want to remain as bus drivers he has worked to ensure that working environment and facilities reflect their commitment too.

Moir is pictured in June 2007 with the then Secretary of State for Education and Skills, Alan Johnson, as FirstGroup became one of the first companies in the UK to sign the Skills Pledge a government-led initiative designed to improve adult learning.

Lockhead treats people at all levels as equals. One day he might be in a bus workshop talking in considerable detail with an engineer about the bus he is maintaining, and the next he might be with a cabinet minister talking about the transport industry. There are no chauffeur-driven cars or executive wood-panelled office suites for this boss. Nor is he surrounded by flunkies waiting to do his bidding. Until the new headquarters opened in Aberdeen in 2009 on the old bus garage site, his office for twenty years was in the garret above the bus depot, with just one secretary sitting next door.

When he leaves his office he travels alone and fends for himself. His mobile and Blackberry are his lifeline. In all but the most important meetings his mobile remains on and set at mute. It vibrates often, he checks the caller, but it remains unanswered.

What many managers appreciate about him is his support and patronage. If he backs a project it happens – and he sticks with it. Initiatives on safety, workplace learning, the environment and rewards for staff would no doubt all be there without his support, but they would not be having as great an impact.

If something is not going well, he has to fix it. It is in his blood. Local managers will be given the chance to get it right, but then, if the problem persists, Lockhead will roll up his sleeves and go and sort it out himself – wherever it might be and whatever the inconvenience. He cannot stand one part of the business letting the rest down.

In the south west of England there were persistent problems with buses and trains. He wanted to find out for himself what it was all about and to get the problems sorted. He arranged a travelling road show whereby he took all his regional MDs to meet local authorities, business leaders and customers. Together they agreed on the issues and worked up solutions. This was no one-off piece of flag-waving. He promised to go back six months later to see whether things had changed. And he went back and back for the next two years and also rolled out the programme to other parts of the UK.

For a man whose secretary once barred him from trying to send e-mails from his Blackberry from fear of what might happen, he is a great enthusiast for technology who recognises the potential benefits to customers as well as the financial rewards it could give the company. Inevitably many of the schemes he promotes are piloted locally and only rolled out nationally once they are proven. Schemes that don't work are quickly ditched, but that does not kill his enthusiasm for the next project to come along.

Sometimes senior managers can hit a brick wall that is obstructing delivery of a key project. They know that if there is no other way of unscrambling things, Lockhead can be a powerful force who will wade in to shift seemingly immovable obstacles.

Lockhead has always been a committed bus man – and this was one of the fears of rail managers when bus companies started moving into the rail industry. But as an engineer he has become just as passionate about the mechanics of running a railway as he ever was about buses. But he is not a man to forget his roots. He has always felt that each job he has held has helped prepare him for his next challenge, and even today he still keeps in touch with old colleagues from his days as an apprentice in Darlington.

Outside First he has helped steer the direction of the Confederation of British Industry through his membership of the President's Committee; he has led the bus industry trade body, the Confederation of Passenger Transport (for which he was awarded an OBE); he sits on the board of VisitBritain; he was the head of Scottish Enterprise Grampian and he has twice been named Chief Executive of the Year in different business awards. He has an honorary doctorate from Robert Gordon University in Aberdeen and an honorary chair in the Department of Geography and the Environment at the University of Aberdeen.

He still finds time to be a tireless worker for charity. His biggest success was as fundraising Chairman for a new children's hospital in Aberdeen. He did not

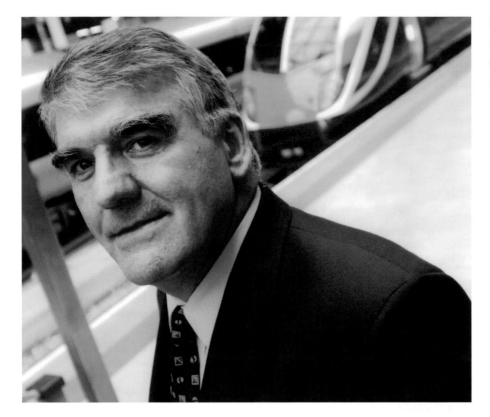

Lockhead poses proudly by one of his new high-speed Adelante 180 trains that were brought into service on First Great Western.

stop until the building fund was oversubscribed by several million pounds. More generally, Lockhead's commitment to children can be further seen by the way the company has forged a partnership with Save the Children.

Finally, in June 2008, it was announced that Lockhead was to be given a knighthood for services to transport. It is a measure of his success that company managers shared his pleasure at this recognition and that his knighthood could have been awarded for many other reasons – such as his work for charity, safety, work-based learning and helping people reach their full potential. Lockhead's regional newspaper, the *Aberdeen Press & Journal*, spoke for many when it recorded:

> *The whole process of honouring Britain's great and good has been discredited in recent years amid allegations that it has been politicised and dominated by the showbiz culture in which a former prime minister liked to immerse himself.*
>
> *In Moir Lockhead's case, this recognition is thoroughly deserved and possibly rather belated. For he is synonymous with the First company which he has helped grow into one of the world's foremost transport*

businesses, with 135,000 employees in the UK and North America. His vision and leadership has brought about the almost unthinkable situation whereby Greyhound buses in America are owned by an Aberdeen company.

Throughout this meteoric rise, the newly-designated Sir Moir has never lost his down-to-earth approach and easy manner which makes princes and paupers comfortable in his company. Today, it is the turn of Sir Moir Lockhead to take a bow and accept royal recognition for a job very well done.

Looking back, it is hard to imagine that Sir Moir could ever have been satisfied just running a municipal bus company twenty years ago.

A changing world

In the early 1970s fleets of buses like this one in the King Street Depot, Aberdeen, dominated city and town centre.

In the heyday of the bus, our towns and cities still worked on historic lines with all roads leading to the centre of town and the marketplace. The bus networks developed the hub and spoke operations that suited those patterns best. Shops, hospitals, places of entertainment, offices and workplaces were all easily accessible.

But progressively after the Second World War, everyone aspired to car ownership and then achieved it, thanks to growing disposable income, the cheaper cars that mass production brought, and engineering technology that slashed both fuel consumption and maintenance costs. In 1950 there were just under two million cars registered on UK roads. Today there are more than 27 million – on average almost every other person in the UK has one. As car ownership soared bus use plunged and tram networks were ripped out to make way for the car.

But road space in old, historic towns and cities cannot expand to meet demand. Even just parked – where they spend some 96 per cent of their lives – those extra 25 million cars on the roads today require an additional 56,800 miles more kerb than in 1950. It is not just the parking that is the problem. Cars are being used more than they used to be. In the last twenty-five years alone the number of passenger miles driven has rocketed by 75 per cent to 424 billion miles a year.

The glorious days of the tram before growing numbers of cars forced them off the roads in the 1950s. Here Bogie Car 34 is turning onto the Hazlehead tramround.

Along the way businesses migrated away from the city centres. Out-of-town shopping centres, multiplex cinemas, business parks, universities, government offices and even hospitals all sought greenfield sites that users could get to easily by car – and where they would find plenty of parking. While that suited the motorist, it was a nightmare for bus networks and their passengers. For bus services to work effectively there has to be a critical mass of both passengers and destinations on any route. If a shopping centre was on the edge of town for example, a bus heading towards it from the city centre could only easily serve passengers from that segment of the city. Everyone else would have to take two buses to get there and two home – not an attractive proposition and one that hastened the spread of the car.

Conversely these out-of-town destinations undermined the commercial heart of some cities, reducing the potential passenger base for bus networks and the importance of traditional bus stations. There was even one case in a First operating area where the health authority built a brand-new Private Finance Initiative (PFI) hospital on a greenfield site miles from anywhere that was not served by any bus route. It then boasted that it had built the biggest car park in the county (which it has since expanded) to serve it. Unfortunately not all staff, patients or visitors had a car. First rose to the challenge and created subsidy-free services that run nearly twenty-four hours a day to the hospital, peaking at services every eight minutes at key times. A consequence of the extra cars on the roads has been the decline in UK bus and tram travel – down from

16,445 million journeys in 1950 to 4,613 million at their lowest point in 2004/5. Since 1990 the core local transport users, the lowest income group, have increasingly had access to cars too. In 1991 just 27 per cent of households in this group had a car, by 2004 the figure was 46 per cent.

Trends in home to school transport have been worsening too. In the fifteen years to 2004, the proportion of 5- to 10-year-olds going to school by car jumped from 27 to 41 per cent, while the percentage of 11- to 16-year-olds arriving by car rose by more than 50 per cent – from 14 to 22 per cent.

We also live in a world where motoring costs – until the recent fuel price rises – have been falling while public transport fares have been rising, thanks to huge rises in wages, fuel, insurance and staff pension costs that have impacted heavily across the transport sector. At the same time countless local authorities have pandered to car owners rather than see trade driven away to a rival nearby community. This has kept city centre car parking charges artificially low,

Aberdeen's Castlegate in the early 1980s.

Midland Scottish buses at Allandale.

Bus shelter demonstrating real-time information.

encouraged excessive on-street parking, stalled the introduction of bus priority measures, and locked public transport as well as cars into the vicious cycle of steadily worsening traffic congestion.

In the mid 1980s, when bus deregulation arrived, many local authorities were only too happy to get shot of their municipal bus services which had presided over decades of decline. The routes of publicly owned bus services were subject to political interference and councillors' postbags. As a result they meandered crazily to meet the wishes of the local complainant rather than the needs of the greater community. The outcome: uncertainty for customers who wanted familiarity, as well as longer and more frustrating journeys. This helped drive people towards the car. And public transport was always the last in the queue when the council was doling out money for investment.

Privatisation of bus services changed that. The figures speak for themselves. By 1990, as services were settling down in the private sector, there were just 73,000 public service vehicles on the roads. Today that figure is 100,000 and the average age of those vehicles is down to 7.8 years – perhaps the youngest fleet Britain has seen in a generation.

Londoners and the city's commuters have been some of the most faithful public transport users over the decades. It has been not so much a matter of choice but practicality. The roads were too crowded and car parking too limited and expensive. Even today fewer than one in ten people arriving in central London in the morning peak comes by car.

As London has grown many London workers have been priced out of the capital or live further out because they prefer the quality of life. As a result commuting by train has spread further and further from the capital. Even in Bristol, some 120 miles from London, peak morning trains can often be nearly full with travellers commuting to London when they pull out of the city. More than 70 per cent of all train journeys start or finish in London and an average of 451,000 people commute by train into the city in the morning peak.

Privatisation in 1996 gave Britain the fastest-growing rail network in Europe in the following decade in terms of both passengers and freight, with rail travel running almost at the levels of the post-war peak in 1946 when the car was not an alternative. In the ten years to 2006, passenger kilometres shot up by 42 per cent to just below the 1946 record of 29 billion.

Over the same period passenger journeys climbed by 43.6 per cent, with 130 million more journeys a year than in France. Only Germany, with a 40 per cent higher population and a much greater network, carried more. Meanwhile, freight traffic by rail bounced back into fashion, carrying 50 per cent more than a decade before. This increase – far greater than expected at the time of privatisation – had a knock-on effect on the creaking infrastructure, on jobs and on keeping environmental pollution in check.

The railways employ over 170,000 people either directly or in supporting industries. The industry contributes about 0.5 per cent of total UK carbon

One of First's London fleet passes Nelson's Column in Trafalgar Square. Unlike the rest of the UK, these are contracted services and Transport for London insists the buses must all be red.

Brunel's great station at London Paddington, where First operates both inter-city and commuter services. It also runs a service to Heathrow Airport.

dioxide emissions, compared to 21 per cent for road transport, with average CO_2 emissions per passenger running at half the level of a car passenger and a quarter of a domestic aviation passenger.

But one cannot look at how UK transport has had to adapt to changing lifestyles without looking over the Channel to see how investment has changed the profile and performance of public transport on the continent. Over the past thirty years the road and rail systems of Europe have been transformed. Investment has poured in, creating high-speed rail links across France, Spain, Germany and Italy.

France's TGV network serves 150 cities and holds the world speed record of 320 mph. Currently it aims to boost normal network speeds from 300 kph (186 mph) to 350 kph (217 mph). Tunnels are being bored through the Alps and the Pyrenees to boost fast services to Italy and Spain. Already the Thalys high-speed trains link Paris to Belgium, Germany and the Netherlands, while all major German cities are served by the high-speed ICE trains that also cover parts of Austria and Switzerland.

First operates freight services through First GBRf.

Spain has spent €21 billion as part of a fifteen-year €108 billion project to transform its rail network. The aim is to have 6,200 miles of high-speed track in Spain by 2020, meaning that 90 per cent of the population will be no more than thirty miles from a high-speed station. The new high-speed Madrid–Barcelona service makes the 410-mile journey in two hours and thirty-five minutes, nearly halving the journey time. The Barcelona line is to be extended to Perpignan in France, making the Catalan capital just four-and-a-half hours from Paris. Work to join Madrid and Lisbon is under way. In 2007 new electrified lines connected Madrid to Valladolid and to Málaga, slashing journey times and doubling passengers on the Málaga line, and growing them by 75 per cent on the Valladolid line.

The Italians have committed themselves to a €28.8 billion network of high-speed lines involving the Rome–Florence, Milan–Naples and Turin–Milan–Venice lines. Journey times on the new Rome–Naples service have been cut to an hour.

Meanwhile the UK currently has no domestic high-speed lines and there are no plans to build any, despite the country being the inventor of the railways and having natural railway territory. The international fast link from London to the Channel Tunnel did not start construction until 1998 – four years after the tunnel opened. A fast line was available from central Paris to the very portals

A French TGV high-speed train.

A high-speed German ICE train.

Eurostar.

of the tunnel from day one. The UK's high-speed link was only fully opened thirteen years after the Channel Tunnel first started serving passenger trains. New high-speed domestic services taking advantage of the international track were unfortunately not able to start at the same date as the government had not ordered the new trains in time.

On the roads of Europe, British visitors continue to marvel at the network of efficient, high-speed motorways criss-crossing the continent, both those already built and those under construction. The fact that many are tolled is accepted because journeys are demonstrably faster, more reliable and more comfortable. The last new motorway in the UK was announced by the British government in 1992 and opened at the end of 2003 as the tolled M6 link – essentially a West Midlands bypass. Pretty much everything else done on the roads has been widening.

Across Europe the story in towns and cities has been impressive. There has been massive investment in light rail schemes, underground systems, bus fleets and traffic management. Even airports have pioneered massive transport interchanges. Both Amsterdam and Paris offer powerful examples. Charles de Gaulle Airport has fast, frequent 'RER' Crossrail-type services stopping directly under the airport, while a massive underground TGV station whisks passengers away on the high-speed network. An automated light rail system operating about every two minutes connects the different terminals.

But what chance has there been of transport policy evolving in the UK when there have been ten transport secretaries in fewer than twenty years – from Malcolm Rifkind, John McGregor, Brian Mawhinney, Sir George Young and John Prescott through to Stephen Byers, Alistair Darling, Douglas Alexander, Ruth Kelly and Geoff Hoon? Each one has wanted to review their predecessor's policies and has then been faced with a Treasury that has stonewalled on funding for anything that looks strategic or visionary. What's more, there has been no cross-party agreement on some of the fundamental issues facing the UK.

Crossrail has been given the go-ahead many times since it was first mooted in 1974, but thirty-four years later not a centimetre of track has been laid. The visionary Thameslink 2000 project providing cross-London north–south rail links was so called because it was intended to be finished by the start of the new millennium. Work only started in 2007 and completion is years away.

The private sector has squeezed as much performance as it possibly can out of the limited infrastructure it has to operate on. To raise its game still further it needs the visionary programmes and investment that other European transport operators have been given by their governments.

Growing up

If Grampian Regional Transport (GRT) was to secure its future through expansion it had to hunt for new acquisitions. Lockhead recognised the benefits of getting in at the early stages of a privatisation process. Here was a one-off opportunity to acquire businesses that were often virtual basket cases at knock-down prices. No one but their own managers, an asset stripper or a company like GRT with a track record of success would have dreamt of taking them on.

Almost all had been neglected by their local-authority owners. They were run down, and their fleets were tired, old and lacked investment. Managers and staff alike were demoralised and had no experience of running a commercial business. Along with the rest of the industry, they chased a declining market downwards while the passengers aspired to car ownership as vehicles became cheaper and more reliable.

GRT had already turned around its own performance; it had learnt how to bring together the normal business skills of operations, policy and finance artificially separated by local authorities; it had learnt the importance of investment, looking after staff, stripping out costs, delivering what the customer wanted, operational performance and promoting its services.

If GRT could get the financial backing and deliver similar changes, it would be well placed to turn other companies around. The break-up and privatisation of the Scottish Bus Group (SBG) which was the trigger for GRT's privatisation created a new opportunity for Lockhead and the management team. Legislation prevented them from buying SBG's nearby businesses, but the same constraints did not apply to Midland Scottish Omnibuses Ltd, the SBG company that had depots in Alloa, Balfron, Bannockburn, Larbert, Linlithgow and Oban along with 772 staff and 282 buses. So just a year after their privatisation, this was to be GRT's first big crack at an outside bus company – and one which would more than double the size of their operation. It was a major challenge and it taught the new managers a lot of lessons.

To prepare for the new assault GRT reported in May 1990 that the company had secured a £20 million loan facility from the First National Bank of Boston (with the Bank of Scotland participating) to provide finance for the acquisition of other bus companies, particularly those being disposed of under the SBG privatisation programme.

But this new acquisition was not going to be easy. GRT had to pay £8.5 million for it and Lockhead remembers that Midland Scottish was still losing

Grampian Regional Council – Ember Red Band-Leyland Atlantean in use sometime after regionalisation in 1976.

£1 million a year. 'People told us we had paid too much for it,' he said. 'It was losing money because it was a public-sector operation. Their view was that buses were in decline and they had stopped investing. Everyone lost direction and the management team was planning its own buyout.'

But this acquisition shook the GRT managers a bit as it took them far longer to turn into profitability than they had hoped. Nonetheless they learnt a lesson which they have applied to every single acquisition since. GRT knew what needed to be done but this first time they wavered. Instead of going in and ruthlessly applying their own proven formula in all circumstances, they listened to the existing team when they said they could do it better another way. GRT found out the hard way that local knowledge could not always deliver more than their own formula. In future GRT would not doubt its own formula for success.

As Lockhead put it: 'Any future acquisition had to have a clear methodology to drive out waste.' At Midland Scottish 'we listened and were persuaded when told that things couldn't work even though they had at Aberdeen. It set our plans back months. In every acquisition after that as part of the due diligence we produced an action plan for recovery. All were losing money and lacked investment. We had a target margin of 15 per cent – we wouldn't get that in three months but we would be making a profit.'

At Midland Scottish there was some difficulty in engineering and turning around the old public-sector culture. This was reflected in GRT's next annual report, which announced:

> *Serious problems were encountered with vehicle maintenance where neglect had resulted in a high incidence of premature failures of major engineering components. This problem has been tackled and, although largely overcome, has resulted in an ongoing build up of work.*
>
> *All staff have responded well to this challenge although the new culture of a wholly independent company has yet to seep through and there is still evidence of the old nationalised sector regime which will have to be addressed effectively over the coming months.*

But this acquisition fine tuned the formula that GRT rolled out over the coming years with all new companies it acquired. It was called the nine-week programme. All five of the top GRT management team would go in as a hit squad on day one to take over the company. Then they would quickly

Moir Lockhead and his team after the acquisition of Midland Scottish in 1990.

pull back, leaving one of them behind until a longer-term succession could be arranged.

Staff and unions would be motivated and brought on side, new uniforms were introduced, an employee director was appointed, cost reductions and new efficiencies were introduced, any management and back-office redundancies would be quickly tackled and an investment programme outlined. Soon the workforce would see that their company now had a future and a clear focus.

As managers at Aberdeen and the newly acquired Midland Scottish company worked hard to consolidate their achievements and deliver profit and growth for the company and introduce new changes, they little realised that a whirlwind was to hit them in 1993. In the space of just three years the company bought bus operations in Northampton and Leicester, the East Anglian Eastern Counties operation and SMT (the Edinburgh and Lothians company) and Lowland Scottish, floated GRT and then merged with Badgerline. Just six years from starting out in the private sector Grampian had gone from a 225-bus operation and 600 staff to one with 5,600 buses, 20 companies and 14,500 staff.

The flotation

Five years after GRT went private the company was floated on the London Stock Exchange, on 5 May 1994. When dealing started three million GRT shares changed hands on that first day, with the price rising from 161p to close at 171p.

By then the company's value had rocketed tenfold from the 1989 original £5.5 million purchase price to £57 million. Hundreds of staff who between them had a 10 per cent free stake in the company had made anything between £10,000 and £100,000.

The decision to go public was not an easy one, as Sid Barrie, then the company's legal adviser and now commercial director, remembers. While the flotation would give GRT access to capital for further acquisitions there was a risk the company could be gobbled up by a predator in the marketplace. Barrie clearly recalls the dilemma. The First National Bank of Boston and Bank of Scotland had been lending GRT the money for acquisitions, but there was always the risk that 'they would run out of the appetite to lend'. And that would leave GRT without the ability to seize further opportunities in the marketplace. The very flotation that would give them access to capital would leave them open to predators.

Unlike many other flotations, said Barrie, this was not about shareholders wanting to cash in their stakes in the business, but a question of access to capital markets that would allow the company to make further acquisitions and grow the business.

The flotation documents of the time highlight a combination of company strengths, including a good relationship with local authorities in the company operating areas:

> *This combined with the high level of employee involvement through the ESOP [Employee Share Ownership Plan] and the high quality of the company's product, leaves the company well positioned to bid for any privatised bus companies. The business also has the additional strengths of management with a proven acquisition record, a geographically spread portfolio of operations focused on city centres, commitment to technology and a large modern fleet.*

The trading floor of the London Stock Exchange as it looked when GRT was first floated in 1994.

The flotation documents advised potential investors that the 'flotation is likely to raise £15m–£20m in new money which will leave the company with net cash and well placed to fund further acquisitions'. The same documents describe some, as it turned out, rather modest targets for the new public company. It 'has set itself the target of becoming one of the top 5 UK bus operating groups'.

While the company was highlighting its commitment to shareholders in terms of investment, quality of service, city centre operations and broad geographical

A set of the original documents that the management and employee buyout team used to persuade Grampian Regional Council to sell their bus company.

spread, all of which it continued to deliver, it also saw a role for local authorities. 'The main thrust of our strategy here is to persuade local authorities that the bus is the key to solving their city's congestion problems', the flotation documents record. Sadly, to this day many local authorities have been demonstrably unable to play their part.

The flotation was a tense time for the directors, and then just before the big day itself disaster struck. The leading City adviser on the flotation, Barry Stubbings, was found murdered in central London. His killer was never caught. Even as the police were trying to trace Stubbings' final movements his fellow advisers were telling the GRT board that the float must continue. It was what Stubbings would have wanted.

Just a year after GRT's flotation GRT and Badgerline got together. The story is typical of the sort of alliance that could be made in the young and pioneering days of privatisation. Lockhead and Trevor Smallwood, the Badgerline chief, were speaking at a conference in Edinburgh. They had already forged links at the Confederation of Passenger Transport, the bus industry trade body of which Smallwood was President – shortly to be followed by Lockhead.

During the conference coffee break the two men started catching up with each other about their respective businesses. 'They were having real trouble with their margins while ours were growing,' recalled Lockhead. 'We decided we could see the advantage of creating scale at a time when it looked as if the competition was breaking away and we each said we would get our advisers to take a look at it. The next thing that happened was that we were meeting to talk about people issues.'

People and places. Neither Lockhead nor Smallwood was keen to move to the other's HQ, so Smallwood and finance stayed at an old farm in Weston-super-Mare while Lockhead and operations stayed in the bus depot at Aberdeen. The two sides would meet at a new London office and boardroom just off Harley Street, where they were to be plagued by patients ringing on the bell thinking they had arrived at a nearby clinic.

A name for the new business was less easy. It was no good calling it GRT/Badgerline or vice versa for two reasons – neither bus man wanted the other's company to go first or liked the mouthful of a merged name. Choosing something else went down to the wire. In the end, as they were brainstorming it round the table, someone said, 'We'll just catch the first bus that comes along.' So FirstBus – later to become FirstGroup when train franchises were won – was

Examples of the Badgerline fleet which revolutionised bus travel in parts of south west England. These smaller vehicles were popular with passengers and were able to run more frequent services.

born. A logo and colour scheme which included the colours of both companies followed twenty-four hours later and the new Chairman, Trevor Smallwood, and the new Chief Executive, Moir Lockhead, signed them off.

The actual process of merging the two companies was a complex one. Separate meetings were held of the shareholders in each company within hours of each other to approve the merger, before court hearings in Edinburgh and London. Then on Friday 15 June 1995 the listings of the two companies were cancelled on the Stock Exchange. FirstBus was born and shares in the new company started trading the same day.

The terms of the merger reflected Badgerline's market capitalisation of £168 million and GRT's £97 million, based on the 3 April 1995 share price of 133p per Badgerline share and 253p per GRT share. Shareholders were to swap their shares on the basis of one Badgerline share equalling one FirstBus share and one GRT share equalling 1.9 FirstBus shares.

The net result was that Badgerline shareholders would hold 63.6 per cent of the new company and GRT 36.4 per cent. The new board told shareholders: 'Following the merger, FirstBus will be the second largest UK bus company. The geographic fit between the two businesses is excellent and this, together with the complementary management styles of Badgerline and GRT, provides scope for enhanced efficiency and a more effective market presence.'

In particular the board identified some key benefits, including the following:
Increased purchasing power: The board expects that the combined vehicle, spare and engineering parts and fuel costs of the enlarged group will be some £95 million per annum. To extract cost savings, most of

Like GRT, Badgerline was one of the pioneers of low-floor buses, which made bus travel so much easier for mothers with young children and buggies, and for the elderly.

*FirstBus' purchasing requirements will be pooled and major supplier
negotiations centralised.*
Operational efficiencies: *Badgerline uses group-level trend analysis
techniques to monitor costs and efficiency whilst GRT employs detailed
benchmarking reviews on its group companies to enhance operating
performance. These techniques are complementary and the board of
FirstBus believes that the application of both techniques will be an
effective tool in improving operating margins.*

The new team outlined FirstBus' structure to shareholders:
*FirstBus is a Scottish registered company and will have its headquarters
and head office function at Badger Manor near Weston-super-Mare.
The Chairman, Trevor Smallwood, and the group finance director,
Tony Osbaldiston, will be based at Badger Manor as will FirstBus'
finance and administrative functions. The Deputy Chairman and
Chief Executive, Moir Lockhead, and the group commercial director,
Robbie Duncan, will be based in Aberdeen at GRT's existing offices
and will have day-to-day responsibility for the operating divisions.*

The existing operations would then be merged into three operating divisions: Scotland, north of England, and south of England and Wales.

The merger of Badgerline and GRT was not easy to start with. People were
branded as either Badgerline or GRT and local managers watched closely to see
which would become the dominant force. Some managers did not fit in with
the more forceful GRT style and were dispatched quickly. (One in particular
believed that instructions from board directors did not apply to him. He was
soon on his way.) Other jobs were carved up into regional fiefdoms so operations could be managed effectively and egos massaged.

Recalling those years in the London office in Weymouth Street, Smallwood
said that in the main Lockhead was in charge of operations while he did strategic development. They had always needed to think ahead to the next development and future growth. He had looked at Europe but they could never get the
right value. Other avenues explored included the Rio de Janeiro Metro and
trains and trams in Melbourne. First was not prepared to bet the family silver
on the deals and was proved right. Another British company won one of the
Melbourne tenders and had to limp away wounded a few years later.

Grampian Regional Council sign the deal to sell its bus company. Flanking Dr Geoff Hadley, convenor, are Moir Lockhead and finance director Robbie Duncan.

But then Smallwood's young son was run over by a car and his leg badly damaged. This injury meant Smallwood had to spend more time at home, which was not consistent with having to jet around the world identifying and developing new business opportunities. He saw that Lockhead had a good sense of where he wanted to take the company and decided to let him have his head. To this day Smallwood remains a major shareholder in the group and has watched developments closely.

When the companies merged, Badgerline had a more recognisable brand with an image of the animal splashed across their buses. It even made its way onto the company notepaper, with a drawing of a badger crawling onto the page appearing at one side. In one spirited act of defiance after the merger, someone at Badgerline's old headquarters ordered a last batch of notepaper showing the badger's backside disappearing off the page. It took longer to re-move the animal from the company's west country bus fleets. Years later local managers were still clinging desperately to the old livery.

The merger brought the new combined company into the big league and operations running from Cornwall to the north east of Scotland. This new force in the transport sector now had the critical mass to strike out at bigger targets – in the bus sector, in the railways and overseas. In the next two years alone it would make massive bus company acquisitions in London, Manchester and Glasgow and win its first rail franchise in its own right.

The new terminal at Bristol Airport doubled capacity at a stroke which opened up the region to a wide range of new destinations.

Soon after the merger First dabbled in two rather exotic diversions before making a very profitable exit. As the company grew in confidence, it decided to look at two other markets: running airports and operating services in the Far East.

In November 1997 First bought a 51 per cent stake in Bristol Airport – then the thirteenth largest in the UK with 1.5 million passengers a year. With forecasts of rapid growth in regional aviation, Bristol desperately needed a new terminal and a backer committed to expansion. This was the company's first dip into the aviation market and, as always, it was looking to see whether, if the venture was successful, there was scope for creating an airports division for the company.

The new airport terminal that First built opened in 2000, doubling airport capacity at a stroke and making the city a popular regional centre to fly from. But it was becoming clear that creating an airports division was a non-starter.

Even to become a bidder for some airport management contracts, companies had to demonstrate that they were already running several large airports. As for buying other airports, prices were starting to go through the roof and First decided to get out of the market.

So in December 2000 the London *Evening Standard* was able to report: *Bristol International, one of England's largest and fastest-growing regional airports, has been sold to a Spanish and Australian consortium for £234m. Transport operator FirstGroup and Bristol City Council put the airport on the market earlier this year.*

FirstGroup acquired its 51 per cent stake in BIA in 1997 for £40m and has invested a further £40m in a new passenger terminal. Its proceeds from the sale will be around £137 million, including repayment of £36m of debt. 'The disposal of our stake in BIA is in line with our strategy to focus on our core transport activities in the UK and US.'

Less than six months after buying its stake in Bristol Airport, the Aberdeen-based company made its first move overseas. And it went to the other side of the world to do it. All eyes were on Asia and the chance to share in the continent's expansion, and the First board wanted to join them. First took a 26 per cent stake in New World First Holdings to run 88 bus routes criss-crossing Hong Kong. Heading the project for First was former CentreWest MD Peter Hendy, who went on to become the Transport Commissioner for London. On the ground the top man was Mark Savelli. The joint venture introduced 226 new air-conditioned double-decker buses with a further 222 entering service the following year. Passenger numbers grew quickly and the company was confident it would win more routes.

Then in the summer of 2000, just a year later, the group announced: 'On 15th May the group disposed of its 26 per cent shareholding in New World First Holdings to the majority shareholder for £38.7 million, giving a profit of approximately £14 million on our investment over the 18 months since trading began.' Once again the board had decided that there was never going to be a Far East division for First, and with North America now on board it would stick to its core businesses and strengths of UK Rail, UK Bus and North America.

There remained a single one-off in the group: its Croydon Tramlink operations. First acquired this interest when it bought its first London bus business

One of the first new trams in London for nearly 50 years. The Croydon Tramlink, operated by First as part of a PFI package, now carries some 26 million passengers a year.

CentreWest in 1997 for £54 million. The bus operator was part of the PFI consortium that delivered the project for a twenty-four tramcar service between Croydon, Wimbledon, New Addington and Beckenham which opened in May 2000 and now carries over 26 million passengers a year.

The Badgerline story

It was the merger of Badgerline and GRT that was to give First the synergies and strength to deliver the empire that was to follow. The two companies and their leaders brought different management styles, geographical spreads and skill-sets to the table.

The Badgerline background is as remarkable as GRT's. Badgerline boss Trevor Smallwood was a man who lived and breathed buses. It ran in the family. His father was traffic manager at Mexborough & Swinton, his uncle an inspector, two aunts were conductresses and another relative was a trolley-bus driver. In his school holidays young Trevor worked at the depot, steam cleaning the insides of the vehicles.

It was no surprise then that, after his A-levels, he became a management trainee at Yorkshire Traction, which gave him the grounding for a career in the National Bus Company. By the time bus privatisation came along, Smallwood was down in the south west of England as Managing Director of the 400-bus and 800-employee Bristol Country Bus, which operated out-of-town services into Bristol and urban services in Bath and Weston-super-Mare.

He was already making a big impression as the largest exponent of mini-buses. In Weston-super-Mare, for example, he was able to exchange eighteen large buses for forty-two minibuses and offer near five-minute frequencies instead of half an hour. Higher revenues paid for the extra staff involved and they were popular with passengers.

With bus privatisation on the horizon Smallwood saw the new opportunities it could offer. He persuaded seventy managers and staff to invest in a buy-out. He was so ahead of the game that he was just a week behind the first bus company in the UK to be privatised – and that was a month before the deadline for public-sector companies to open themselves up for competition.

Smallwood reckoned that by going early he could buy at a cheaper price and be better placed to pick up other companies as they were sold off. And so

Trevor Smallwood, one of the pioneers of bus privatisation, was the founder of Badgerline and later the first chairman of FirstGroup.

it turned out. Initially he stuck to the south west, picking up Western National in Plymouth and Cornwall before buying Cityline in Bristol and Midland Red West.

South Wales Transport and Brewers were next, before the company snapped up Eastern National in Chelmsford and Essex. By 1993 it was time to float the company and the share prices showed the staff how successful they had been.

Smallwood recalled how, before the first privatisation in 1986, a driver in Bristol had come to him and said he only had £1,000 but wanted to put it into the new company. The driver was staggered to see that the share price after just seven years showed that the £1,000 was worth £260,000. He was by no means alone. One bus inspector brought his wife into the garage to ask Smallwood what the share price meant for his valuation. His startled wife told Smallwood: 'I only married him for his free bus pass.'

As with GRT, the flotation allowed Badgerline to accelerate its acquisitions. In 1994 it bought both the PMT Group in Staffordshire and the Wirral and Yorkshire's dominant bus operator Yorkshire Rider. This made the company the largest bus operator in the UK with 3,900 buses, some 10,700 employees and a turnover of £223 million, generating a profit of £17 million a year.

It was not easy to reach pole position as Badgerline had some very acquisitive competitors – with Stagecoach and GRT both growing fast too. By now the big operators had to start thinking about market share as the regulatory authorities were keeping a sharp eye out for signs of market dominance.

By the time GRT's Moir Lockhead and Smallwood met for a cup of coffee on the margins of an Edinburgh conference, both realised that if they were to look for major growth it had to be outside the bus sector. Rail privatisation was on the horizon, and privatisation and new market opportunities were growing from Australia to South America and Europe.

The two chief executives recognised that each had a different approach. First had been targeting municipal bus companies and Badgerline the traditional National Bus Company operations around the UK. If the two were to join forces and would only be allowed 25 per cent of the market between them, they would want to make sure it was the best 25 per cent – and that meant Manchester, Glasgow and London. Big challenges like these would be easier to tackle if GRT and Badgerline combined forces. A combination of Badgerline's strategic approach and wanting to get into markets early coupled with GRT's

Examples of the Badgerline fleet illustrate the range of liveries and vehicles in use at the time.

focus on post-acquisition growth made sense. They would become a major force in UK transport and deliver good shareholder value.

But even while the two companies were planning their marriage, Smallwood and his team were planning to repeat with rail what they had done with buses – namely to get in early, buy cheaply and get a head start on the competition. In the event the opportunity fell into their laps. City investment group 3i were backing a management buyout team at what was to become the Great Western franchise and were looking for a private-sector transport operator to beef up the team. Smallwood, who already had designs on Badger rail franchises, agreed to take a 25 per cent stake in the company and a seat on the board in return for £1.5 million investment from Badgerline.

In the event the management buyout won the franchise, which started operations in 1996. As one of the first tranche of three passenger franchises to be launched, there was not too much competition and the price and terms were much more favourable than later bids. Later, when 3i wanted to exit the

A Great Western high-speed train in the livery of the management buyout company, in which Badgerline had a stake.

franchise, FirstBus had been formed and Smallwood picked up the whole franchise along with North West Trains, which it had acquired along the way.

But 3i were also backing a later management buyout team for London's Liverpool Street franchise out to Essex and Suffolk. Again they wanted transport sector support, and by this time Badgerline and GRT had merged to become First and the old Badgerline bid team was there to help First win its first rail bid in November 1996. By now the new company had set up a London office just off Harley Street on the fringes of Marylebone, where both Smallwood, the new Chairman, and Lockhead, the Chief Executive, had an office.

First ScotRail services cross some of the most stunning scenery anywhere in the United Kingdom.
Here the Oban–Glasgow train has just passed Kilchurn Castle between Loch Awe and Dalmally,
and is crossing the River Orchy where it enters Loch Awe.

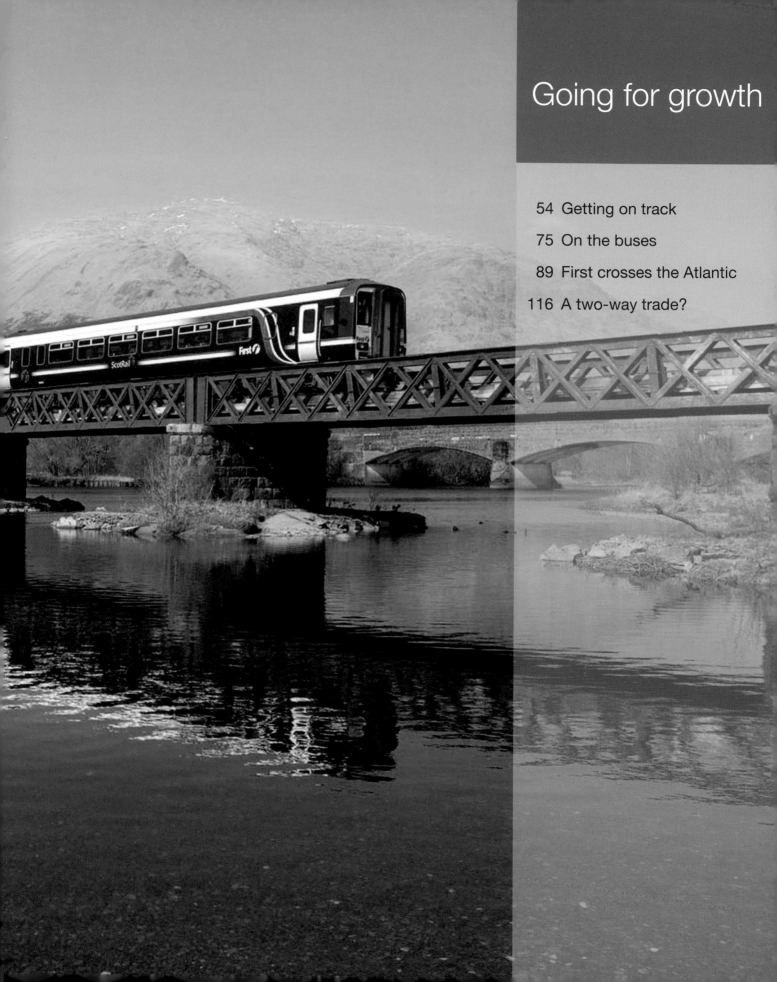

Going for growth

Getting on track

The old British Rail was a much unloved and unappreciated institution – until the time came to privatise it. It had been starved of investment by successive governments and suffered swingeing cutbacks inflicted by the infamous Dr Beeching. And the trade unions dished out regular, punishing national rail strikes to the luckless passenger. Critics claimed that the organisation was so unbusinesslike that if a service became too popular they would price people off it through hikes in fares rather than run extra trains to meet the demand. It was said that managers cared more for the operational challenge of running the service than for the passengers they carried.

An inter-city service in the old British Rail livery.

In the early 1990s John Major's Tory government signalled that they were going to privatise the railways – something that Mrs Thatcher never dared. Members of the government feuded publicly about the best way of doing it – for example whether regional companies should be responsible for managing the track and signalling their trains ran on, or whether the national infrastructure should be maintained separately. In the end they settled on carving up train services into twenty-five different operating companies running on track rented from a separate national infrastructure provider.

By the time a White Paper was published in the summer of 1992, the British public, often resentful of change, was ready to leap to the defence of the status quo – despite the fact that it was British Rail. Trade unions and managers had a field day whipping up the opposition, media and passengers against the plans and the trench warfare continued right through to the introduction of the first privatised services. The threat to safety was a common theme – even though the privatised British Airways had already proved it was essential for a private operator to demonstrate how much safer they were than the public sector. (Rail's safety record also improved further after privatisation.)

Critics were right in one respect, though. The industry was to become too fragmented. What had been one rail business suddenly became twenty-five passenger-operating companies, three train-leasing companies, three rail-freight companies and a national infrastructure company that hived off maintenance to a range of newly created companies. With each company operating in a tight contractual framework, reconciling who was contractually responsible for a train being late became a lawyers' paradise.

A classic example of a one-company-runs-all advantage was railway signalling. Before privatisation signallers took a pragmatic, common-sense approach. If an express train was approaching your sector you gave it priority over regional and commuter services. As for freight trains, running more slowly than all other services, it did not make sense to let them have priority over everyone else as everything would then have to run at the speed of the slowest train. That logic went out of the window after privatisation with late-running freight trains signalled in front of an express. No wonder the passengers were angry.

For bus companies like First the bidding process for the new passenger train companies ruled out much of their entrepreneurial flair and they had to agree to put on a regulatory straightjacket. For example the cost of leasing the trains had already been fixed by the government, the track access contracts for the trains had already been signed, and perhaps as much as 90 per cent of the timetable had already been determined before companies started to bid.

The weaknesses of the contracts the government had pre-negotiated on train operators' behalf with Railtrack, the infrastructure provider, soon became apparent. It can best be illustrated by comparing a train operating company to a householder. As a householder, if you need maintenance work done on your house you decide exactly what work you want carried out and how much you have to spend. You then get quotes from different builders and agree a price and starting date – holding back the final payment until work is finished.

It was all rather different with Railtrack. You had no choice about who carried out the work, the price of it or when it would be done. They took your money at the outset, then decided how much of it was going to be held back for shareholders and which region the remainder was going to be spent in and when. Worse still, a train company had no idea whether the work would be carried out at all and there would be no breakdown of costs. It was great for Railtrack but a pretty raw deal for train companies and their passengers.

First was a little slow in getting into rail franchise. There had been considerable internal thought and debate about this new market. On one side, it was felt that the profit margins in a heavily regulated rail business would not be as high as in the bus market while, on the other, it was recognised that leasing rolling stock was less capital intensive than buying buses.

In November 1996, nearly a year after the first franchises had been awarded, the Aberdeen company was named preferred bidder for its first rail business:

the Great Eastern Railway franchise running commuter services from London's Liverpool Street out across Essex and Suffolk. Its 576 railway carriages travelled 6 million miles a year to 60 stations on 164 miles of route. At the time, the then First Chairman Trevor Smallwood said: 'We are looking forward to unlocking synergies between our bus companies – Eastern National and Eastern Counties – in the region and Great Eastern. People already travel by bus to catch the train and we will be looking at more rail links.'

By the time First Great Eastern handed back the franchise in 2004 at the end of the franchise period, it had turned a £40 million-a-year subsidy from the government into a £10 million premium for the taxpayer and was the only operator in the region not to be receiving a subsidy.

But its ending had caused a storm in the industry and the region. Despite having earlier pre-qualified the company for the bidding process for the second generation of franchises to be rolled together for the region, the Strategic Rail Authority (SRA) excluded First from the whole bidding process on the grounds that it had not filled in the application form properly. At that stage there had been no commercial or financial proposals put to the SRA by First or any other bidder.

Commuters were up in arms. Some 3,000 bombarded the SRA in support of First Great Eastern – an unprecedented reaction from customers. An opinion poll carried out by MORI on behalf of FirstGroup found that just 3 per cent of passengers backed the SRA's contentious decision, an overwhelming 85 per cent of passengers saying the company should have been allowed to bid. The poll went further and showed that support for the company's rail services was running at twice the national average – 79 per cent approved of the train frequencies (against 45% nationally), 73 per cent of punctuality (37%) and 43 per cent of value for money for fares (24%).

In the House of Commons the Colchester MP Bob Russell said:

What I and thousands of other rail users are saying is that it is completely unfair that the SRA has banished First Great Eastern from the shortlist. The SRA has refused to give verifiable reasons for excluding First Great Eastern. That has prompted some to ponder whether the SRA decision has more to do with the settling of old scores by senior members of the SRA against First Great Eastern than with what is best for a public railway service in the east of England. I am told that the SRA decision is without precedent.

First Great Eastern: one of the first trains operated by FirstGroup when it took over the franchise.

First went to the High Court to challenge the SRA on how it had come to its decision. The company won the first round and the SRA was obliged to release the formula it had used in taking its decision. But then First decided to drop its challenge. A company spokesman was reported in the Colchester *Evening Gazette* at the time as saying: 'The SRA has decided they're not reinstating us and we've got a broader business to consider. It's very difficult for an operator. There's no appeals process and we're in the hands of the SRA – its decision is final.'

Meanwhile FirstGroup had another plan up its sleeves – it decided to re-enter the competition for the new Anglia franchise by buying a company that had already prequalified: GB Railways, owners of Anglia Trains, Hull Trains and freight operator GB Railfreight.

The *Evening Standard* reported on this:

First Great Eastern has been 'saved' after its parent company bought out its Liverpool Street rival for more than £23 million. First Great Eastern (FGE) which had been stopped from bidding for the right to run all services in the East of England from October 2004, has now bought one of the firms that is in the running – GB Railways, owner of Anglia Railways, the express company operating to Norwich.

Peter Northfield of First Great Eastern said this week: 'This is a complete turnaround from a few weeks ago. However we suspected

*something was in the offing when the main company gave up challenging
in the High Court against the decision to exclude us from bidding. Now
it is by no means certain we shall win the franchise at the end of the day
after the rollercoaster this has all turned out to be, but we all feel it is
game-on again at FGE.'*

In the end it was not enough and First failed in its new bid for the Anglian
franchise, but its rail operations were expanding elsewhere and the company
was soon to become the biggest rail operator in the UK, even winning several
rail businesses off the company which it had lost out to in East Anglia. Poetic
justice!

In the early years of rail privatisation Railtrack were making more money
for its shareholders by sweating the assets and extending the gaps between
maintenance. While in the short term this made lots of shareholders very
happy, the state of the track started to look less and less fit for purpose. It all
culminated in the Hatfield rail disaster, when a GNER express train hit a curve
on 17 October 2000 and the track failed. The ensuing high-speed derailment
killed six people and led to speed restrictions lasting more than a year on many
parts of the network as Railtrack tried to get to grips with the state of its track.

These failings were to become critically important for First because in March
1998 it had announced it was acquiring Great Western Holdings for £104.8

One of First GBRf's contracts is to haul
coal to fuel-hungry power stations.

A First Great Western regional service hugs the south Devon coast on the main line between Plymouth and Exeter.

million. The company already had a 25 per cent stake in the business. Unfortunately the track the trains were running on was some of the oldest and least modernised on the network – and the company was dependent on Railtrack to put it right. Although Great Western had been one of the first train operations to be privatised, it had been a management buyout and had been cushioned from some of the cultural shocks that other rail operations had received from day one. Alison Forster, a senior manager in the company at the time who later went on to become MD, explained:

We thought we had been privatised by the management buyout but they had not done a complete review of the business, which First did as soon as they arrived.

It seemed a brutal business – every job in the organisation was looked at on the assumption that we did not need it. But it was very good. We had been a fatter organisation than we needed to be – and less responsive. The structure changed enormously and, at HQ, we lost easily 10 per cent of our staff. But, at the front line, the numbers of drivers went unchallenged.

Forster recalled that the changes all came quickly in the first year, and as a result of them everybody had real clarity and became much more customer focused. Managers had a shorter chain of command and a real feeling of control. First managers were all over the company in that first year, understanding the business and safeguarding the investment. Once they felt comfortable with the way the business was performing, they took more of a back seat.

But there were some other major cultural changes in the company too. Typically, across the rail industry at that time there were a number of old-school managers who turned up their noses at the thought of being managed by a bunch of busmen who, they felt, had nothing to teach them. That attitude did not last long. If those managers could not adapt they were asked to find a career elsewhere.

Forster remembers some other changes. Because the original Great Western sale had been a management buyout, staff had been encouraged to take a stake in it. Something like 67 per cent had done so and stood to benefit enormously by FirstGroup's purchase of the company. In the mess room at the Swindon headquarters of the railway company no one would have dreamt of looking at the financial pages before First bought the company. Suddenly they all were, recalled Forster. And if there was a big daily movement in the share price they would all ask the Managing Director why. Their stakes were not small change. Forster recalls a rash of second homes overseas and new boats appearing across the company.

If the staff were happy, the same could not be said of the relatively new Labour government. The unhappy Deputy Prime Minister John Prescott put his view:

This takeover is yet another example of the privatised railway making individuals into millionaires at the expense of the passenger and the taxpayer. It is further proof of the need for a new rail authority, to ensure the railway system is run in the public interest.

Last November I scrapped the previous government's guidance to the franchising director, to promote privatisation, and told him to put the passenger first. I am pleased that as a result of these new instructions, he has been able to negotiate a £75 million package of improvements for passengers of Great Western Trains and also Great Eastern and North West Trains. The package includes 32 new coaches on Great Western, a week's free travel for monthly and longer-term season-ticket holders, stiffer penalties for late trains, and more bus/rail through ticketing.

Prescott mentioned North West Trains. This franchise was part of the Great Western Holdings package that First was buying. And it was a disaster. A badly negotiated contract, it was losing money and performing an appalling service. When First took the company over it had to inject new talent, private-sector discipline and investment into the company quickly. In time the train service moved from being the worst performing regional one to the best. First was sorry to lose it in 2004 when the final part of the government programme to split the franchise into three different rail companies was completed. (Some routes went to a new all-Wales franchise, others to a new northern franchise, with the remainder hived off to the new TransPennine Express franchise.)

The new trains that First agreed to take on for the First North Western franchise were to be manufactured in Birmingham by Alstom and were part of what the French manufacturer hoped would be a new generation of trains to serve the newly privatised companies. However, introducing them was an exhausting process involving a multitude of teething problems for both Alstom and Railtrack. Unbelievably, the infrastructure provider did not know the physical

A First Great Western high-speed train in its old livery.

dimensions of its own system. Each train has its own 'kinematic envelope'. This is the space it takes up if it is to clear any trackside object, whether it is leaning to take a bend, travelling through a tunnel, running alongside a station platform or passing under a bridge. Since Railtrack did not know the dimensions of its own infrastructure, it was in no position to sign off that this new train was safe to run on it. It was months before it was able to license the trains for passenger travel.

A higher-speed 125 mph version of the trains – called Adelante – was ordered from Alstom at the same time for use on First Great Western routes. These had similar teething problems and never became as popular with passengers as the old high-speed train still in service today after more than thirty years. In the end, FirstGroup handed some of them back to Alstom as they proved too expensive to lease. Even a single thirty-year-old 125 mph train costs around £1 million a year to lease under the privatisation leasing regime.

By 2003 the passenger rail franchises that had come to market first were due for renewal and the government were starting to think about consolidation of franchises. First had helped demonstrate to them that if you had only one train operator using a single London main-line station there was much

more flexibility in the use of platform and track. And flexibility meant extra capacity on lines that were already bursting at the seams at peak times. But, as operators found, putting back together what the government had torn apart was not so easy. In some renewed franchises three train companies were merging into one, each with a different operator. And that meant different cultures, working practices, terms and conditions – often for doing fairly similar work. That is a recipe for industrial dispute and discontent and it can be several years before everyone settles down together.

Another complication for First was that it, inevitably, felt compelled to bid for franchises coming to market both because it would help grow the company but sometimes also because it was defending contracts it already had. This was an expensive and time-consuming business. The process took months and cost First around £3 million per bid, and each bid involved up to two hundred people. And if it was a franchise that it was already operating, that took managers away from their day job of running services for customers.

While these were difficult and unsettling times for staff in the rail companies up for tendering, they at least knew that at the end of the day their jobs would remain. Like many railway people, their loyalty was to the part of the network they were working on rather than to a remote parent company.

Meanwhile First's problems with the SRA were continuing. The Thames Trains franchise was due to finish in 2004. Its trains shared London's Paddington Station and some of the routes outside the capital with First Great Western. Merging the two franchises would be good news for passengers, creating extra capacity and more services in an integrated operation. However, since First Great Western's franchise did not expire until 2006 passengers looked as if they might have to wait an unnecessary two years before they could see any benefit.

FirstGroup did a presentation to the SRA on the benefits that amalgamation could offer, and was later stunned to find that the SRA had ignored the passengers' interest and was doing a quiet consultation on awarding Thames Trains owners a two-year extension to its contract without opening up the process to other bidders. Despite a commitment to consult with interested parties, the SRA had left First off the consultation list – even though the company shared routes, track and Paddington Station with Thames Trains. First could find no conceivable reason for this behaviour and had to appeal over the SRA's heads direct to the Department for Transport to be included in the process.

A First Great Western high-speed train standing behind the rather sleeker looking Adelante. Passengers, however, still prefer the extra space they get in the older train.

A day in the life of a high-speed train

It's just after 4 a.m. when the depot driver climbs up into the cab of First Great Western's first high-speed train of the day at Plymouth's Laira depot. Over the next twenty hours it will travel almost 1,000 miles and carry around 3,300 passengers.

During a typical day a single train makes three journeys to London, two to Cardiff and one to the Cotswolds, spending the next night in Swansea. A similar story is played out each day by the forty inter-city trains on these routes.

During the day the train will have six different drivers, five different train managers and a total of nine different catering staff on board. Overnight it has been topped up with 1,000 gallons of water and 2,000 gallons of diesel fuel, a nightly regime for a train that consumes 2 gallons of diesel for every mile travelled.

Since it arrived at the depot a few hours earlier, six engineers have spent ninety minutes carrying out their three-nightly safety and maintenance programme as well as checking the driver's and train manager's logs for any reported defects. The train is cleaned and vacuumed.

But now, checks done, motor fired up, signal at green and clock showing 4.20 a.m., the train pulls slowly out of the maintenance shed and heads for Plymouth, where the rest of the five-strong crew will join it.

The train's day

0420	Leaves Plymouth's Laira depot
0522	Plymouth–Paddington (arr. 0938)
1015	Paddington–Cardiff (arr. 1220)
1255	Cardiff–Paddington (arr. 1501)
1551	Paddington–Worcester (arr. 1758)
1815	Worcester–Paddington (arr. 2036)
2115	Paddington–Swansea
0032	Arrives Swansea

Once there, station staff put up seat reservations and stock the buffet ready for the pre-dawn 5.22 a.m. Plymouth to Paddington via Bristol Temple Meads service. When the train pulls out around twenty-four Paddington-bound passengers are on board, with another hundred or so making shorter journeys to points between Plymouth and Exeter.

It has rained overnight and the rainfall monitor on the Devon coastal cliffs near Dawlish has triggered an automatic landslip alarm at the Swindon control centre, resulting in a 20 mph speed limit for the section. By the time the train reaches Bristol it is the peak of the morning rush hour. All 480 seats will soon be full.

Since the train was built commuter patterns have changed, with London office workers living ever further from the capital. When the train pulls out of Swindon, still an hour from London, there will not be a spare seat. About a thousand people will have travelled on this service for their morning commute to London or a city en route.

Into Paddington at 0938 with time for a train tidy up, buffet restocking and a crew change before the train sets off for Cardiff at 1015. This is a quieter journey with a different passenger profile. Most of the two hundred on board are leisure travellers using the standard class carriages. The majority of this journey is on high-speed track and, signals permitting, the Cardiff-bound train will be doing 125 mph by the time it has left the capital.

Key facts

On an average day a high-speed train:

- travels nearly 1,000 miles
- spends nearly 20 hours at work
- carries some 3,300 passengers
- burns 2,000 gallons of diesel fuel
- has six different drivers
- is more reliable than when built nearly 30 years ago.

At Cardiff, once the customers disembark, the train heads for the sidings and the cleaning crew climb aboard to give the carriages a quick once-over. During the journeys themselves staff have removed the most obvious rubbish like newspapers and food wrappings. Over the course of a day the train will be cleaned or tidied several times and many sacks of rubbish removed.

At 1241 the train is signalled back to the station ready to make up the 1255 service to Paddington. The driver who brought it down is rostered to take it back. On an average day the driver will do one long-distance return journey or one shorter return journey plus a local return leg. This is another quiet time of day with around three hundred passengers on board for the journey.

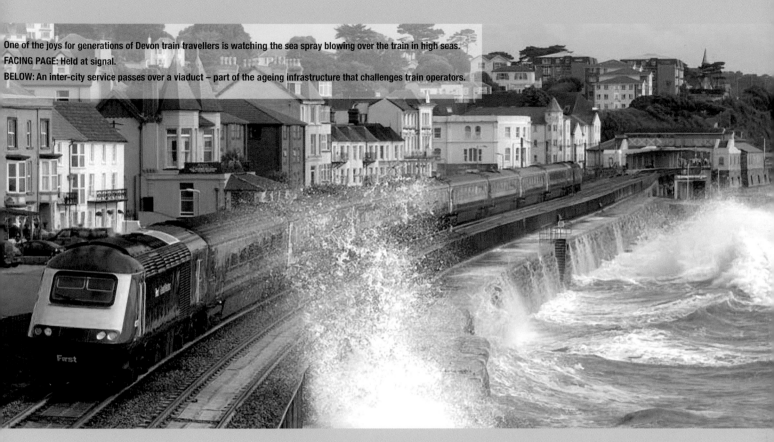

One of the joys for generations of Devon train travellers is watching the sea spray blowing over the train in high seas.
FACING PAGE: Held at signal.
BELOW: An inter-city service passes over a viaduct – part of the ageing infrastructure that challenges train operators.

Back at Paddington at 1501 there are fifty minutes to prepare for the busy evening ahead. It's time for a route change and a new crew drawn from the 2,000 on-board staff the company employs.

This time the train is off to Worcester. It's a difficult run because much of it is on single track – it's common to be held up by a train coming in the other direction, an unattractive prospect for the six hundred people on board. To make matters worse, it is a tight turnaround for the driver with just a seventeen-minute gap between arriving in Worcester and loading up with passengers for the 1815 back to London.

This is another popular train, again carrying six hundred passengers in the course of its journey. For the driver it's an opportunity to keep up route knowledge on this stretch. If six months pass without making this run, the driver is not permitted to make it again without further familiarisation.

Each train
- travels more than 300,000 miles a year
- can go up to 125 mph
- has 480 seats.

Back at Paddington at 2036 the train has another crew change for the journey down to Swansea. This 2115 service is a popular one. Five hundred people make their way home –

business people after a long day in London, leisure travellers returning to Wales and people taking shorter journeys home after meeting friends after work.

After nearly twenty hours on the move and 3,300 passengers later, the train arrives at Swansea at 0032 for a few hours' rest before starting all over again.

Eventually, announcing that FirstGroup would be the preferred bidder for the two-year extension in November 2003, the SRA confirmed First's version of events:

> *The SRA has been in discussions with Go-Ahead Group regarding a two-year extension to its current franchise since Summer 2002. In September 2002 it separately received an unsolicited proposition from FirstGroup to combine Thames services with Great Western services from 2004. The SRA invited FirstGroup and Go-Ahead Group to submit proposals for a two year franchise on 10 April 2003, having received a Section 26 direction from the Secretary of State for Transport, enabling negotiations to start.*

The early benefits to passengers of the First proposals soon became clear when the SRA spelled them out just before Christmas 2003. They included these:

- up to 20 per cent increase in rush-hour seating capacity on Reading to London Paddington fast services
- a 7 per cent improvement in the percentage of trains arriving on time across both franchises
- average journey time savings of five minutes for the majority of London to Oxford services through the use of faster and more comfortable 125 mph trains
- extra express services for the south west with the restoration of a three-hour journey time between Plymouth and London
- more seats on London to Bristol and South Wales trains, with the reintroduction of high-speed trains on the route.

These improvements all came two years early because of FirstGroup's lobbying.

Even while these changes were being planned and implemented, Moir Lockhead was galvanising his rail team into a bid for the mammoth ScotRail franchise with its 75 million passenger journeys a year, 344 stations, and 2,100 services a day. It would be fair to say that the rest of the management team did not quite share his enthusiasm in the early days. The incumbents, by general consent, had done a good job. At first the chances of dislodging them with a killer bid did not look high, but Lockhead was determined. The company's headquarters were in Aberdeen, First was the biggest bus operator north of the border and ScotRail ran around 95 per cent of the trains operating in Scotland. A win would make First a very important player in Scotland.

Parts of the rail industry were stunned when, in 2004, the SRA announced that First had been named preferred bidder for the franchise. Announcing the win, the SRA said it was 'a critical milestone in delivering better rail services for Scotland. It follows a healthy competition among the bidders, all of whom put in strong bids. It should bring about an overall improvement in punctuality with further passenger benefits including better customer information, greater security through enhanced CCTV facilities, and improvements to train and station cleanliness.'

First appointed a woman to run the franchise: Mary Dickson (now Grant), a Scot, who had worked on the bid for the business. A tough, determined, hands-on operator, Dickson took a grip on the franchise from the start. Under her reign the franchise was named Public Transport Operator of the Year in 2006, there was a reduction of over 50 per cent in delays that could be attributed to the operator – despite a franchise commitment of a 2 per cent a year reduction – and investment of £40 million in station improvement.

The franchise has proved so successful that the Scottish government extended its life by three years to 2014. Announcing the deal in early 2008, Transport

Road journeys can never match the glorious sights that Scottish train travellers have around them.

Minister Stewart Stevenson said: 'The extension is down to the success of First ScotRail in delivering levels of performance above and beyond those set out in the original franchise agreement.'

Another important rail win for First preceded the ScotRail announcement, and that was the contract for the brand-new franchise TransPennine Express. The contest for this was hard fought, and it spanned a couple of years as the SRA dithered over what exactly to put in it and the relationship with the new northern franchise, which swallowed up all the remaining northern England regional services.

First bid for TransPennine with Keolis, a French transport operator that remains a partner in the franchise today. Under Vernon Barker, who had been MD of First North Western until the SRA split it up, the franchise has gone

One of the new First TransPennine Express train services that have transformed train journeys between the east and west coasts. A glorious escape from the clogged motorway journey.

A First TransPennine Express makes one of its stops at Grange-over-Sands.

from strength to strength. The idea for the franchise was a sensible one. Road links across the Pennines depend on the very crowded M62 motorway and yet there was plenty of spare capacity on the rail link that connected the conurbations of Manchester and Liverpool with Leeds and Newcastle.

But no one in their right mind would want to take the old train services. Rolling stock was old and unreliable, and boarding the trains was by one tiny door at each end of the carriage. Trains were delayed in run-down stations as passengers fought to get on and off. First's plan was to invest in a complete fleet of new trains which would have faster acceleration, and would be more comfortable and easier to get on and off. That would be backed up by a massive station improvement programme and a focus on performance and reliability. The Managing Director also recognised a new market for his passengers: services linking with Manchester Airport, the north's biggest airport.

The company took over TransPennine in 2004. Its new fleet of fifty-one Siemens-built 100 mph trains arrived in service on time in 2006 and within the £260 million budget. The thirty stations on the route have been given a £12 million makeover and all front-line staff attend customer services courses and can complete railway operations qualifications (NVQs).

The results have been impressive. Passenger numbers were set to reach 23 million in 2008/9 compared with just 13.4 million at the start of the franchise, while customer satisfaction figures were the highest of all inter-city train companies at 88 per cent. Delays and cancellations fell by more than half and 92 per cent of trains achieved their punctuality and reliability targets. Meanwhile the trains serving Manchester Airport saw a 43 per cent rise in passengers in three years.

It is not surprising that those achievements resulted in an HSBC Rail Awards grand slam in 2006, when the company walked away with more awards in one year than ever before achieved by a single rail company. The company was named Rail Business of the Year, won the Rolling Stock of the Year award, the Business Manager of the Year (Vernon Barker, MD) and the Marketing Campaign of the Year, and was highly commended in the Train Operator of the Year and Internal Communications sections.

Even as TransPennine was carving out a reputation for itself, First's rail franchise bidding team under the direction of finance director Dean Finch was feared across the industry. The company was winning a higher percentage of its bids than any other operator and taking competitors' businesses off them at a time when it had still more franchises to defend.

A day in the life of a rail franchise – First Capital Connect

It's 5 a.m. At sidings from Cricklewood to Cambridge early drivers from First Capital Connect are collecting their trains ready to take south-east commuters to work. Before the day is out they and their colleagues will have carried 150,000 passengers and travelled 71,000 miles.

Early as it is, these are not the first staff of the day. The earliest clock on at 3 a.m. Some of the company's trains have been running throughout the night, linking London with Luton and Gatwick airports. Monitoring the services twenty-four hours a day is the West Hampstead control centre manned by staff from First, who look after the train service, and Network Rail, responsible for track and signalling.

be safe, clean, on time and comfortable and there when they want them.

Also reporting for duty for the early trains are some of British Transport Police's twenty-four police community support officers paid for by the rail company. Their patrolling of trains and stations has been a major factor in cutting anti-social behaviour by 44 per cent since First took over. And now that vandals, like everyone else, have to buy tickets – thanks to increased ticket checks – the troublemakers have moved away.

Meanwhile at seventy-eight stations around the network, station and booking office staff are ready to open. The Croydon, King's Cross and West Hampstead control centres are changing shifts ready for the morning

there to speed up service recovery. Most of First's own failures at the start of the new franchise were down to inherited rolling stock problems. Thanks to the new maintenance regime, trains go up to 25 per cent further before an incident that holds up a train for five minutes or more.

Dawn is breaking, and drivers have collected nearly 150 trains from their depots and sidings and brought them out into morning service. Before they go home tonight each train will have travelled up to 800 miles and carried some 1,600 passengers.

Platforms are getting steadily busier as the morning commuter peak approaches. These days commuters are not just going into London but to business centres outside the capital. And they mix with the suitcase-laden passengers heading for Gatwick and Luton airports. Traffic has grown hugely on these routes since First took over and started working closely with the airport operators. At Luton, where First has just started operating comfortable shuttle bus services between station and airport, rail revenue to Luton is up 27 per cent in less than two years. On Gatwick services it is up 19 per cent.

The morning peak is past now and the trains settle into their daily average of four return journeys each. Across the franchise area the company's training academies are getting busy. It takes over a year to train a driver and another thirty-five will be needed when extra new trains come into service.

First took over the services in April 2006 with a mission to transform the Thameslink and Great Northern railways. The account of one day shows how it is improving services on the only main railway lines to run services right across London, from Bedford to Brighton, as well as connecting stations from Cambridge and King's Lynn with the capital.

With commuter rolling stock designed for shorter journeys, the best that staff can hope to achieve is that passengers' journeys will give them less to worry about. The trains will

peak. At each computer screens plot the exact location of trains. Staff are ready to intervene should an incident look like having a knock-on effect on other trains. Only a quarter of delays to trains are caused by First Capital Connect failures. More than half are due to Network Rail's infrastructure failures and 15 per cent are caused by other operators.

Today everything is running well. The lights are out in the incident room in Hertford House – only after an occasional incident like a failure of overhead electrical wires do managers rush

The customer is central to everything First Capital Connect does. Equipping staff with the right tools for the job is key to their success so it has created its own customer service training programme. To date 199 front-line staff have received national vocational qualifications and BTECs. The programme continues.

Customer care is exemplified at the company's flagship station, the newly revamped St Pancras International, where First has recruited new passenger-focused staff, many of them with languages needed to

First Capital Connect on Blackfriars Bridge, one of the more scenic images of London. There is never a shortage of passengers wanting to use First Capital Connect for business or to spend a weekend sightseeing in London.

help international passengers connecting with airports or Eurostar – and in future those visiting the 2012 Olympic Games, for which the station will be a major transport hub.

At the company's headquarters the management team has 2,100 company staff to look after – including 550 train drivers, 500 customer care and ticket office staff and 250 revenue protection staff.

Meanwhile, in the daytime, the train depots are looking comparatively empty as most trains stay in service after the morning peak. Only trains due for heavy maintenance or in for repairs are over the pits. Looking after the rolling stock is a vital safety service and an expensive one. Each carriage has 32 brake pads and there are 620 carriages. That's 20,000 brake pads at £35 a time. A single wheel set costs up to £7,000.

With the evening commute home out of the way, the last staff are leaving some of the

smaller stations by about 9 p.m. The first trains have headed back to the depot by around 7 p.m., although most will stay in service until between 9 p.m. and 10.30 p.m.

Work is just starting to pick up in the depots with cleaning and depot maintenance crews arriving to prepare the trains for tomorrow. Every train will have its exterior

washed and be given a good clean inside. Every month it will also go through a rigorous deep-cleaning programme, while every eight days a maintenance team will carry out regular inspections.

The trains are all electric so at least there is no refuelling to do – just a huge cheque to write out to Network Rail.

The team was about to claim another scalp – this time a franchise that brought together the services of Thameslink and Great Northern. These services were often overcrowded, unreliable and lightly managed. It was notoriously easy to travel for nothing on some trains because many customers felt there was no point in paying for a ticket if no one was going to check you had one. Stations and trains were dirty and queuing at the ticket office could be a frustrating business.

Once again First had a woman running the franchise: Elaine Holt, another hands-on manager. She was a woman who, like Mary Grant at ScotRail, took no prisoners in her determination to give passengers a good service. Although this attitude might surprise an outsider to the industry it shouldn't. If financial targets are to be met revenue has to grow and therefore passenger numbers have to rise. That will only happen if performance improves and passengers feel they are being looked after.

Commuter services are never going to have that 'wow' factor with the public. Commuters simply want their trains to be comfortable, safe, on time and reliable, a luxury that has not always been the case. Holt had to move fast to give passengers their confidence back.

Trains were smartened up and deep cleaned, maintenance regimes were sharpened up, station security was improved. Holt worked the corridors of power to get more rolling stock for a chronically overcrowded franchise and put pressure on Network Rail to deliver more reliable infrastructure. Stations were given a makeover and staff provided with customer service training. A big boost was the opportunity to move out of the shabby old King's Cross Thameslink station into the totally revamped St Pancras, opening up direct links for millions of people to the Eurostar network and the continent.

And if there were not enough police to deal with vandalism on the routes, you could pay for them yourself. In a new piece of railway innovation, Holt told British Transport Police she would fund twenty-four police community support officers provided they worked full-time on the franchise. Anti-social behaviour has fallen 44 per cent as a result.

The big win for First was undoubtedly Greater Western, the consolidation of three franchises: Wessex Trains, Thames Trains (by then First Great Western Link) and Great Western itself. In the space of eleven years the staff had all gone from working in one big organisation – the old British Rail – to being divided into three and then finally being brought back together again. In the

The interior of a refurbished First Great Western high-speed train serving passengers on the new franchise.

These re-engined First Great Western power cars are performing better than at any time since they were built – and they bring major fuel savings and environmental benefits too.

meantime terms, conditions, customer loyalties and operating practices had all been changed and now had to be stitched together again. To win the new franchise First had to demonstrate its commitment to investment, and within the first two years it had completed a £200 million total refurbishment of the entire high-speed fleet and all its power cars. But it also had to commit to paying the government a huge premium for the privilege of running the services – £1 billion over ten years.

The management strain of simultaneously binding three franchises together again, running a major investment programme and making the economies necessary to pay both them and the government premium soon told. First Great Western reliability started to suffer, and as the cracks showed it became clear that there was no simple solution. First recognised that radical change was needed – it was not going to have one company letting down the brand. Typically it poured in managers and money to help get it right. Some £29 million of additional investment was agreed with the Department for Transport and top managers were brought in to plan and deliver the recovery.

Sadly the much deserved poor headlines hid the many benefits that First has delivered on the Great Western routes over many years. In all the years since privatisation it has suffered from having to operate on some of the oldest, most underinvested and most fragile infrastructure on the network and from using high-speed trains that came into service in the 1960s. Just getting the services running on such a Cinderella network has been an unsung triumph.

What has been delivered should not go unrecorded; if the team had had the benefits other franchises faced of modern track and newer rolling stock, who knows what might have been achieved? Nonetheless, since privatisation it has created a business that runs more high-speed trains than at any time since the line was built, with many key stations better served than ever before and with up to four high-speed trains an hour in each direction – a frequency many towns in the UK can only dream of.

At peak times the company has been running as many trains as the network can accommodate, with a third more services and 50 per cent more passengers than when it started. Despite being built in the 1960s, the trains are now more reliable even than when they were first built with the engine replacement programme making them twice as reliable still – and more environmentally friendly. By juggling platform, timetable and fleet the company has added an extra three million seats a year into and out of London Paddington to cope with rapidly growing demand.

At the same time the company has pioneered new operations systems to build on performance and introduced a groundbreaking joint control room with Network Rail to ensure the company is able to recover quickly from any incident.

The story overall of the company's rail operations – which also include Hull Trains and the company's freight arm First GBRf – is a proud one. It is a tale

A Hull Trains express which runs regular high-speed services to and from London. It is extremely popular with passengers and wins awards for its customer service.

of investment, growth and performance improvements with a constant focus – as elsewhere – on safety and customer service. First's Rail division has breathed fresh life into flagging services, introduced new and innovative products, bored into new markets and brought a new pride and dynamism to the sector.

On the buses

Bus services were in their heyday in the 1950s. Trams and trolley buses were being phased out, but the motor car was just a dream to most families. Journeys by bus and coach peaked at 13,225 million a year in 1955 when there were 3 million cars on UK roads. Today there are 27 million cars, and bus journeys plunged to 4,231 million journeys a year at the bottom of the cycle in 1998/9.

In the golden age of the bus, workers in big factories or other organisations often used to have their own works special buses which whisked them direct from their suburb to their factory gate in the morning and then home again at night. For the rest there was no need for bus lanes on roads gloriously free of traffic. Journey times were predictable, you could hop on and off between stops, and travel was more enjoyable provided you did not venture up to the smoke-filled top deck.

Aberdeen in the post-war years: tram tracks still run down high streets, cars are still a novelty and the bus is king. Here a Daimler CWA6 utility 150, followed by a Walker Bodied CVD6 on South Market Street.

Since those heady days it has been a long spiral of decline for the bus. Not only did passenger numbers plunge, but buses had to fight for every bit of road space as car numbers soared and roads became more congested.

The local-authority bus service became the poor relation of the council's operations. It was bottom of the queue for investment in new fleets and it was at the whim of councillors' postbags. Bus routes became more and more complex as they adapted to meet the idiosyncrasies of individual voters' angry letters. Routes became slower and less attractive to passengers, who opted more and more for the car. The bus manager had little clout with the local authority over the provision of bus priority measures and also had to battle for the sort of innovations and changes that any other manager would take for granted.

It was against this history and backdrop that bus deregulation came about. Margaret Thatcher's Transport Secretary, Nicholas Ridley, published a White Paper in 1984 proposing to free the industry from competition restrictions and repackage the National Bus Company into bite-size chunks that could be transferred to the private sector. Importantly for the future of FirstGroup, bids from employees would be welcomed.

The Transport Act of the following year put it all into effect. The impact was mixed. In many parts of the country commercially minded public-sector bus chief executives built successful companies, taking advantage of the new freedoms.

Costs were reduced, service frequencies improved as more and smaller buses were introduced, and new routes came in. Meanwhile local-authority support for the industry (at 1994/5 prices) crashed from £974 million a year before regulation to £279 million ten years later.

Not all went smoothly. Bus wars broke out in some parts of the country as new operators fought for market share. That was particularly seen in some of the big northern England metropolitan areas.

Scotland resisted privatisation and the sale of the Scottish Bus Group subsidiaries did not begin until May 1988, but by August 1991 the process was all over. The delay in Scotland caused serious market distortion. Glasgow was a case in point. The streets of central Glasgow, which had seen ninety buses an hour before deregulation, suddenly had to cope with three hundred or so.

And as across the UK town hall bus operations fell to the private sector, a host of little operators came in to cherry pick the most profitable routes into town, trying to run their buses a few minutes before the scheduled operator so they could cream off the maximum number of passengers for the puniest of investments.

Meanwhile, although most operators were happy to swim along in their own quiet little pond, the bigger fish were circling round, seeking any opportunity to consolidate their operations. And so we soon started to see the so-called 'bus barons' mark out their future territory. Alongside GRT were Badgerline, British Bus, Go Ahead and Stagecoach. While some companies were comparatively indiscriminate in their purchases, GRT focused firmly on urban services with their bigger passenger base and the bigger opportunities for growth – a trait continued today when 75 per cent of First's bus services are on urban operations.

From the outset First (and its predecessors GRT and Badgerline) was determined to innovate and grow the market. Nothing was sacred – from vehicle size and type through to marketing and routes – in the bid to get passengers back. Badgerline, for example, invested in a big fleet of smaller buses that were cheaper to buy and operate and less intimidating.

On the GRT side, right from day one and even before, the company knew that growth was not going to come unless local authorities recognised that they had a duty to public transport as well as car users. Buses needed to have priority measures, covered shelters, pull-ins and access to parts of city centres

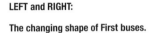

LEFT and RIGHT:

The changing shape of First buses.

that were not open to cars. They also needed councils to use their leverage to limit the number of cars entering the hearts of cities by restricting the number of parking spaces and putting a price on parking spaces, particularly to discourage car commuting. Park-and-ride was already on the agenda.

In the early days GRT was quick to voice its concerns about traffic. In its 1991 annual report it recorded the opening of Aberdeen's Bon Accord Shopping Centre with its:

> 'consequential traffic' congestion problems. This highlighted the effect of such developments on our ability to provide reliable bus services throughout the city. As a result, passenger numbers fell dramatically when congestion was at its worst on Saturdays in the city centre and resulted in traffic grinding to a halt. Despite extreme policing measures to restrict car access to the Bon Accord Centre, the problem of route reliability continues.
>
> It was gratifying to see the Regional Council quickly grasp the problem and undertake traffic flow studies to maximise the potential of public transport by better management of road space. The introduction of improved traffic measures along with bus priorities later in the year is tangible evidence of the working relationship between the company and council members and officials. The jointly sponsored approach to this study to determine the very important role of the bus has helped to generate a renewed interest in providing improved bus travel throughout the Grampian region.

Today's UK Bus division is very different from the local Aberdeen operation. It has 25,000 staff, operates 3,000 routes with 9,000 buses, and carries nearly three million passengers a day. It operates one of the youngest bus fleets in the UK, having invested in 4,000 new buses in just six years and taking the average age of the fleet down to below eight years.

Each of First's bus companies around the UK is a stand-alone operation in its daily operations but with central support for engineering, procurement, marketing and human resources. It also has to bid to Aberdeen for investment in either new infrastructure or buses.

The central core is constantly searching for new initiatives, innovations and opportunities that will encourage more travellers back to the bus and make operations even safer and more efficient. These include working with central

In February 2008 First announced the industry's largest ever order of new buses – 700 new buses worth £100m were rolled out.

LEFT: The Granite City's Union Street, where First buses are part of the scenery.

government, local authorities, manufacturers and consultants on delivering the partnerships that are so important in delivering bus passenger growth. These can range in scale from national down to city and even route-wide improvements. Sometimes development starts the other way round with First trialling an initiative locally and, if it proves successful, rolling it out across the UK.

The list is endless, from the Overground networks (providing simplified routes and turn-up-and-go services with modern fleets), ticketing initiatives, park-and-ride schemes, guided busways, **ftr** streetcar, real-time information, and so on. In these days of congested towns and cities, though, the passenger will see only limited benefits from innovation unless the local authorities are prepared to partner First in delivering change. First has pioneered Quality Partnerships with local authorities across the UK. Some work better than others.

They work best when there is total trust and commitment between the two, with the operator investing in enhanced services and new fleet in exchange for the local authority providing bus priority measures. Often the local authority has to take away congested road space from the motorist and give it to a bus lane in the face of intense local opposition from shopkeepers and motorists. In many cases the operator/authority partnership has to introduce trial schemes to prove their effectiveness before rolling them out more broadly.

Bristol was a case in point. Its economic success meant that driving to and within the city could be a nightmare and buses got stuck in it, like cars. Proposals to run a pilot quality bus corridor into the city centre were vigorously opposed. Shopkeepers felt it would reduce trade and motorists feared for their road space. In the event the initiative was successful and now First is working with the city and developers on a £68 million plan for more.

Central to the success of bus operations is the ability of buses to avoid being stuck in the traffic congestion that holds up everyone else. That has two benefits – it allows public transport users to have more reliable and faster services and it also encourages motorists to switch from the car, thus reducing congestion. In Leeds for example, where motorists caught in heavy morning commuter traffic saw buses speeding by on their guideway and then stopping outside their offices, it was a real encouragement to make the switch. The trick has been to introduce priority measures only at points where traffic congestion can be predicted, such as on the approaches to roundabouts. This cuts down on the road space take and the cost.

A dream operation for First is the sort of business it has in York. The local authority cares passionately about preserving its history and keeping traffic well away from the oldest parts of the city. It has sited park-and-ride car parks and services on all the key approach roads to the city, keeping cars – but not buses – from gated areas at the heart of the city and providing bus priority measures for the fleet. This encouraged First to offer York the opportunity to be the launch city for **ftr** streetcar, a new concept in public transport blending the comfort and stylishness of a light rail system with the flexibility of a bus.

While First's bus companies around the UK have to operate to group customer service, engineering, accounting and branding standards and to pre-agreed contributions to the UK Bus division budget, individual managing directors are given a lot of autonomy in the way they actually run their companies.

Park-and-Ride services prove popular for First customers up and down the country.

An ftr: the innovation from First that offers the comfort of a tram combined with the flexibility of a bus.

After all, they know their customers and markets better than a headquarters staff in Aberdeen does.

This is the way First does business across the company. Local management teams are given the tools to do the job, the support they need in times of problems and the investment funding if they can make a business case for new fleet or new infrastructure. They are then left to get on and deliver. But managing a bus company is not easy and in Manchester – for example – getting 788 vehicles cleaned, fuelled, married up to 788 drivers and out onto the road before dawn every winter morning is a challenge. And that is if all goes well.

With ever increasing traffic congestion, more buses need to be added to routes to keep the same gap between services and it becomes harder to run buses to the scheduled timetable, risking provoking the Traffic Commissioner to threaten to take your vehicle licences away. Then there are the inevitable traffic accidents, vandalism and incidents that make inroads into fleet availability. And as unemployment figures drop other companies are trying to poach your staff, which makes it harder for you to man the buses. Then there is always the risk that the government's vehicle inspectors will make an unscheduled raid to check the state of your buses.

Meanwhile fuel costs are going up, wages are soaring, and insurance and pension costs are rising, making it harder and harder for you to meet your budget commitments. On the way transport ministers change along with transport policy, and there are increasing local-authority challenges to the services you are providing. At the same time head office is urging better and better performance and wanting you to get more passengers back onto the buses.

These are the struggles of bus company management, and sometimes so many of the issues come together that a company can be overwhelmed. Occasionally, by the time that it is possible for Aberdeen to appreciate that radical support is needed, customers have already started to vote with their feet. This happened with First's operations in Manchester, where service concerns forged an alliance between Passenger Transport Executive (PTE), passengers and media that left the local company feeling it was under siege. The issues went way beyond what local management were empowered to deliver and there was no quick fix.

The purpose of this story is to illustrate that running a bus company can be a huge challenge, and that First cares passionately about providing a service that the customer wants to use and will go to any lengths to turn it around. It also reflects well on the PTE and councils that gave First the space and opportunity to deliver. Perhaps the city remembered what First had done to help make the 2002 Commonwealth Games in Manchester such a success – providing ninety-five brand-new state-of-the-art buses worth over £11 million to transport athletes, officials and the media to and from the various venues.

Once the scale of the Manchester problem registered on the radar screens in Aberdeen, Moir Lockhead flew in to meet top PTE and council officials and

Low-floor buses have transformed travel for disabled people.

First was the official transport provider for the 2002 Commonwealth Games held in Manchester.

A day in the life of First in Manchester

It is 4.30 a.m. and the early shift bus drivers are reporting for duty with First's Manchester bus company. It will be a long time before most of their day's passengers will even be waking up, let alone heading out to join the morning commute which starts to kick in at 6.30 a.m. each weekday.

By then most of the 787 drivers due on this morning will be in their cabs as the company gears up to take the city to work, to school and off to do the daily chores. During the day the fleet will serve 190 different routes, carry 239,000 passengers and travel around 95,000 miles.

This is the story of one day in the life of one First bus company in one city. This daily

pattern is repeated at First bus companies across the nation every day. To keep the fleet on the road the Manchester company has 2,300 staff made up of 1,800 drivers, 300 engineers and 200 administrative staff, supervisors and managers in an operation that never sleeps.

For drivers the day starts when they sign on at the depot and pick up their running board with a complete set of instructions for

the day, from route timing points to end-of-route turnaround times. Over the next ten minutes they will look at a chart to see which bus they have been allocated, find it in the huge bus park and carry out the vital 'first use' inspection. This safety check will look for any damage to the vehicle, and ensure lights are working, wheels are sound, brakes are functioning properly and bells and emergency door buzzers working.

Out on the streets the driver will follow the same route throughout the day. Not so much of their time is taken up with fares collection these days, although all passengers' journeys need to be recorded on the ticket machine. Only a third of passengers buy single tickets,

the most expensive option. Half choose to buy all-day or weekly tickets offering unlimited travel throughout those periods. This benefits all passengers since they only have to buy a ticket at the start of the day or week and board much faster for the rest of the time.

Drivers have to monitor their times closely since if they are running more than a minute early or five minutes late the company can be fined by the Traffic Commissioner for failing to

keep to the timetable. Traffic congestion makes it increasingly hard for journeys to stay within time, and bus companies are now having to add extra vehicles on the worst routes to ensure they can stick to those times.

Meanwhile back at the company's depots and the Manchester bus station, canteen staff are preparing the meals that will keep the drivers going throughout their shift. This is the only time in the working day that they get to meet and chat with their fellow drivers.

Also hard at work in the depot is the driver training team. Over the year they will train 360 recruits on courses up to seven weeks long. At the end of it the trainees will emerge with a bus driver's licence and a job on the front line. They will have had not only practical and theory driving tests, but training in health and safety, route knowledge, customer care, security and the cash handling and fares routine.

Back in the traffic office the staff are monitoring bus performance, assigning shifts and ensuring the smooth running of the day's services. Even though only 7 per cent of journeys in Manchester are by bus, the numbers are enormous. Each bus carries an average of more than 300 passengers a day; a busy route can have more than 10,000 a day. Over a day the fleet will carry 240,000 passengers – that's 1.7 million a week and 88 million a year. And the numbers are growing – with non-concessionary passenger numbers rising at 2 per cent a year.

By 3 p.m. most of the early drivers have finished for the day and the late shift will be

Hundreds of new buses like these have transformed services for Manchester bus users.

coming on duty, ready to work through until 11 p.m. or midnight. For most staff and buses, though, it is time to head back to the depot once the evening rush hour is over. For the drivers there is just time to dock their ticket machine module in a depot reader and to pay the day's fares into an automated cash-counting machine before heading off home.

But, while their day is over, for many of the depot crew it is just beginning. Overnight every one of the buses goes through a routine of washing – inside and out – and refuelling, and the driver's log is checked for any failure reports such as a rear light not working or graffiti that need to be cleaned up.

During the course of the day each bus will have used more than 40 gallons of low-sulphur diesel and travelled more than 120 miles, entirely in urban areas and much of it in heavy traffic. Together First's Manchester bus fleet will have travelled nearly 95,000 miles and consumed 31,500 gallons of fuel.

For the maintenance teams life has become a lot simpler. Much of the fleet is almost new with nearly three hundred brand-new buses having been purchased for the company in just two years. This has boosted reliability, raised morale and made the company much better placed to attract passengers back to the bus.

leaders. Soon to follow were the heads of bus operations and engineering, backed up by a support team of managers and operations experts. Ian Davies, one of the company's leading bus directors – who had piloted Yorkshire's buses with huge success – was brought in to lead and deliver the change programme. He quickly changed the company structure, with one managing director put in charge of everything. At last people could be absolutely sure who was running the business. Previously there had been different MDs in different parts of the city with a regional one above – a recipe for confusion. Behind him, Davies recruited a strong operations and commercial team.

Andrew Scholey, who was brought in as Managing Director of First's 870-strong bus fleet after Davies, explained the scale of the changes the company made. Number 1 was the investment in new buses. In 2005 and 2006 some 250 single-deck buses and 18 new articulated buses poured into service in the city – nearly a third of the entire fleet. That was followed a year later by another thirty-six double-deckers. This brought low-floor, passenger-friendly buses across the city, improved reliability and image and boosted staff morale. It did away with the last tired and end-of-life buses serving the city.

Simultaneously the beefed-up management team started rebuilding relationships with stakeholders and getting out to meet everyone, from local councils to the highways departments, the PTE, councillors and MPs. Everyone started working together for the good of the city and its passengers.

The company put a new focus on service reliability. Having a new fleet and tougher engineering quality control helped enormously, but the buses had to be manned at a time when many employers were competing for the same staff. Around a hundred eastern European drivers were recruited, backed up by local recruitment, and staff turnover was reduced from over 30 per cent a year to 21 per cent. (The eastern Europeans were part of the 1,500 mainly Polish staff the UK Bus division has taken on.)

A performance improvement plan was implemented with a dedicated manager and six-strong team assessing the problem services and running times, changing schedules and talking to council highways departments to iron out infrastructure bottlenecks.

But sometimes the company felt it was running just to stand still as traffic growth in the area rocketed 15 per cent in ten years and a rival operator claimed that traffic speed had fallen from 14 mph to 11 mph an hour in just four years. The PTE and local authorities have ambitious plans to turn those round and have bid for massive government funding to support them. First's new management team is in there, giving them every support possible as part of its focus on customer service.

First in Glasgow

If First's UK Bus division is the company's first and favourite child, its Glasgow operations are the jewel in the crown. It is the company's largest bus operator, the test bed for several key new First initiatives, and it is a city where First passengers have a choice of the company's bus and rail services (delivered by the company's award-winning flagship First ScotRail franchise).

The company has more than a thousand buses operating from six depots on a route network that covers 1,523 miles. Every weekday 413,000 passengers board a First in Glasgow bus – to put it in context, that's two thirds of the population of the city itself, although the company serves the broader region too.

In the four years to 2008 the company has invested £41 million in 321 new buses for the city and surrounding region. The company and its 2,900 staff pioneered the Overground network system that has subsequently been rolled out right across the UK. It was nothing less than a root and branch reform of the city's bus network. Each route was looked at in fine detail to test its relevance and whether it was serving the community best.

A bus company nightmare – the fleet gridlocked in heavy traffic. It shows the importance of bus priority measures which separate buses from other vehicles.

As a result a network of simple bus corridors was developed, tailored to serve the maximum number of people and give them the shortest possible routes. Frequencies were planned for just turn-up-and-go levels. Each route was colour branded and the overall network mapped out in the style of the London Underground route map. As a result passenger numbers grew as people grew more confident in the network.

The city pioneered subsidy-free 24-hour-a-day services and introduced get-tough policies against anti-social behaviour on buses, and is now bringing in a whole raft of reforms under Managing Director Mark Savelli, a man with a mission to get more passengers back on to buses – and a man who knows that won't happen unless the performance is spot on.

Savelli has brought bus performance to around the government's 99.5 per cent reliability target and seen his passenger numbers growing at a rate of 2.2 per cent a year as a result. In some weeks growth is running at 3.4 per cent. Achieving these targets is not easy. With Department for Transport statistics showing average off-peak urban traffic speeds falling 4 per cent in just two years Savelli has to add 4 per cent more buses and scheduled time just to stand still. For example on one of his routes (the no. 62) he has had to add a whole

One of First ScotRail's 2,100 daily services.

A First bus in Glasgow leaves Central Station.

hour to the timetable for a round trip to provide a reliable service. In 2001 the schedule allowed for a 192-minute round trip. Today it has to be 246 minutes – and that is even with bus priority measures the local authority has introduced on the route.

To grow passenger numbers he has introduced fast new comfortable express services, and passenger numbers for the routes have shot up by up to 70 per cent in a single year. There are now new dedicated airport links and even night-time special nightclub services. Park-and-ride operations and new walk-on frequency services seven days a week up to 11 p.m. are bringing in new bus users too.

In all these changes Savelli has been helped by the new staff culture which has made them feel more part of the business. And he works closely with politicians, the PTE, local authorities and the communities themselves to make them feel they have a voice in the shape of the bus network, which is then formalised in a route development plan which Savelli is expected to stick to.

Meanwhile on the rail network in Scotland, First ScotRail has been outperforming other train operators (as usual). The company runs 2,100 trains a day across Scotland and carries more than 81 million passengers a year – 19 per cent more than when it won the franchise four years earlier.

First crosses the Atlantic

In the 1990s the UK led Europe – and the world – in privatising public transport. The big operators that had established themselves in those early years needed to expand into other markets as they reached near-monopoly positions in the UK. Other European operators were watching closely. They could see the writing on the wall in their own countries and sought to muscle into the UK market to broaden their experience and prepare themselves for the threats they would be facing too.

Some of the big UK transport companies took the fight back to them, looking at the opportunities that Europe might present – First among them. But the Aberdeen company saw big risks, low margins, over-regulation and some markets that overprotected their domestic providers and manufacturers. On the rare occasions when First did put in a bid it was at a price that reflected the risks it would have been taking, and the company was not successful. But it was a nervous period for the UK winners. In those early years some British transport companies invaded new markets, only to retreat later from some after learning hard lessons.

First Student

The United States was a different ballgame for First. It had been the graveyard for British companies in the past and the City looked twice at any company entering that market. However, First thought it had found a new opportunity that matched its skill-set and experience of dealing with the public sector. It was the school bus market. A deeply fragmented business that was mainly local-authority run, the market was estimated to be worth up to $14 billion a year, and only 30 per cent of the 470,000 buses in service were in private hands. Many of those were run by local 'mom and pop' operations.

American-organised school transportation began in the late 1800s with horse-drawn vehicles borrowed from farmers. But by 1910 some 30 states had school transport programmes in place. And, as the nation's road programme expanded into rural areas – notably in the 1920s and 1930s – motor vehicles were quick to replace the cart.

As the number of school buses increased, they became involved in several tragedies. That made school officials think seriously about developing some tough safety standards. In 1939 representatives from forty-eight states gathered to make recommendations for school buses. That seven-day conference attended by state transportation officials, school bus manufacturers and paint companies set forty-four industry construction standards, including specifications for body length, ceiling height and aisle width. It also introduced the now famous uniform yellow school bus colour – a colour that cannot by law be used for any other type of vehicle in many states of America. It was selected because its contrast with black paint makes it stand out in the semi-darkness of early morning.

There are some 470,000 yellow schools buses on the roads of North America. In many states no other vehicles are allowed to use the same shade of yellow paint.

While today's school buses do not look much changed from their predecessors of thirty to forty years ago, they are structurally very different. The improvements in the past decades, combined with improvements in driver training, school bus maintenance, and school bus operating procedures, have been responsible for the outstanding safety record of school transportation.

Today there are some 470,000 yellow school buses that carry 24 million

Children return home from school in the United States. Their bus service drops them at, or very close to, their homes.

students every school day. Between them the buses travel four billion miles a year and make more than nine billion student trips – making the yellow bus by far the largest form of surface public transport in North America, carrying nearly twice as many passengers as the urban buses (transit services) a year – the latter's total is 5.2 billion. And what's more, they are the safest form of transport around.

In the ten years to 2000 an average of six children a year died as school bus passengers, yet eight hundred are killed every year getting to and from US schools by car, bike or on foot.

Behind the safety figures lies the whole school bus culture – from the vehicle through to its operation and its customer friendliness. First has progressed this to a fine art. The company sees the whole operation as a partnership between school, parent and operator. For it to work the parents and schools must have total confidence that their children are safe in First's hands. To begin with they need to have complete reliance on the vehicle. Built like tanks, they are slow moving, well maintained and replaced every twelve years.

Children are seated high above the ground, well above the point of impact if the vehicle is involved in a collision. Seats are close together and padded so the passengers are cocooned in a moving eggbox, protected from injury in the event of any impact. And in the US other drivers have to stop if the bus is loading or unloading children, to prevent children running out into the path of another vehicle.

As both financial and political pressure was applied to local authorities to outsource those services in order to deliver greater efficiency and financial savings, companies with First's experience were well placed to move yellow bus operations into the private sector. No one knew better how to strip out costs, deliver economies of scale, introduce customer service and new safety standards, and squeeze the best possible deals out of vehicle manufacturers and other suppliers.

The problems facing school boards – and their solution – were summed up by Daniel R. Rawis, superintendent in the parish of Pointe Coupee, Louisiana, who wrote:

Throughout the country, almost all public (state) school systems are faced with challenges; economic downturns, eroding tax bases, reduced state funding, each contributing to an enormous problem of providing educational services to public school systems with diminishing support.

Therefore, each educational system must attack this problem by identifying areas of service that can be delivered in an enhanced and more professional manner, as to provide the same service, or better, at a reduction of the cost. The parish of Pointe Coupee is rural and sparsely populated. Nonetheless, the school system has experienced a unique challenge of providing transportation to its students. Individual bus owner/operator employees have faced daily extremes of finding and purchasing fuel, upkeep of buses with skyrocketing repair costs, cost-prohibitive prices for buses, ever-increasing auto insurance cost, diminishing value as buses age, not to mention reduction of employees' personal credit score as they financed expensive buses on their own personal credit. As a school bus owner/operator, it was no longer a money making enterprise for them. Faced with these challenges, the Pointe Coupee Parish School board realized that the way of the individual employee contract was fast becoming a thing of the past.

What was a problem for school boards was an opportunity for First. It was also a business that was recession and weather proof – children had to get to school whatever the economy was doing, and school populations were rising across the country with the continuing flood of immigration. Also if there is a snowstorm and school districts have to close down, missed days are made up

Yellow buses have to be able to cope with every kind of weather condition – snow is all too common on many of First Student's routes, particularly in Alaska, Canada and the northern United States.

at the end of term. Unlike traditional bus operations where companies face a revenue risk in the event of any economic downturn, once you had won a school bus contract it was yours for perhaps five years as long as you provided the service.

Lockhead and the management team had always played the long game and they had had their sights on their first US target – Ryder Transportation – for many months. The company was 90 per cent trucking and leasing and its 9,500 school buses made up just 10 per cent of its business. First saw an advantage in separating Ryder from its school fleet, which carried 650,000 students daily across twenty-six states.

There was just one problem for First – Ryder's bus division was not on the market. For months Lockhead and Tony Osbaldiston, the then financial director, tried to persuade the company that school buses were not part of their core business. Their persistence eventually paid off in 1999, and First paid Ryder $934 million (via a £238 million rights issue with the remainder by debt) for Ryder's network of 9,500 buses. Along with it came the bonus of small transit and vehicle service companies. Although it was the second largest school bus business in the US, Ryder had less than 3.5 per cent of the 470,000-bus US market. As Lockhead pointed out after the purchase: 'Only one third of the

A day in the life of First Student's Cincinnati operation

Cincinnati has traffic issues just like most major cities in the United States, and school buses may get stuck like everyone else. Schools start at 7.30 a.m., and First Student's Cincinnati operation on the north side of the city starts early. First in, at 4.45 a.m., is the dispatcher who controls the operations on the 150 routes. His job is to get the buses out on time, keeping communication with the Cincinnati Public School District city bus supervisor and radio contact with his fleet.

The early drivers sign in at 5.15 a.m. About 85 per cent are women, many of them single mothers. It is a friendly company with regular social events for the staff, and those who get used to the hours tend to stay. From the dispatcher's window they collect their keys, and confirm that they have their Zonar card and their route sheet. Then they have a 10-minute vehicle safety inspection before they can hit the road. Children are precious cargo

and these checks of brakes, lights, steering, tyres, mirrors, safety exits and equipment are crucial.

The early vehicles, ranging from 72-seaters to 12-seaters, start trickling out soon after 5.15 a.m., battling with early commuters for fifteen miles before swinging off to the Greater Cincinnati area to run against the traffic flow for the rest of the journey. Although the buses have power steering, a 40ft-long, 8½ ft-wide bus weighing 16 tonnes is not easy to manoeuvre.

By 6.15 a.m. even the buses with the shortest journeys are making their way out. Some have booster seats for young children – only a few per vehicle, but they allow children as young as 3 to get to their pre-school groups. They sit close to the driver so an eye can be kept on them. Many of the buses are used for special needs children. The young ones are accompanied by an attendant on the bus.

Each student has their own numbered seat that they use every day – older ones usually at the back and younger ones near the front – and the same driver is on the route the whole year. Even so, sometimes there are problems and children get a verbal warning. If problems persist they are followed by written warnings which parents must sign and return. These warnings are entered into the school's database and forwarded to school transportation. After a third warning a child can be suspended from the bus, a powerful deterrent.

By now the buses are reaching their first pick-up points – the number varies between 6 and 20. For the youngest and for special needs children the stop may be outside their front door. At each stop the driver puts on the flashing lights, a stop sign comes out at right angles to the bus and a 'gate' swings out to prevent children passing close below the driver's line of sight. Legislation bars all vehicles from passing while children are boarding or getting off.

Back at base the dispatcher is getting radio feedback on local traffic conditions from the drivers. A 10-minute delay early on can often be made up, but if traffic gets backed up schools must be warned so they can be prepared for late arrivals.

At the school the drivers arrive at a staffed bus zone that keeps children away from other vehicles so they get to their classrooms safely. For the driver there may be educational runs, sports trips or inter-school journeys before the school day is over. If not, it is time to return the bus to the terminal until the end of classes, unless the journey is long.

At the terminal a new class of driver candidate is going through the eight-week driver training programme. There are over 235 people on the payroll, including 170 drivers, 40 attendants, 7 mechanics, 3 trainers, 5 dispatchers and 9 office staff. The management team are evaluating the latest company equipment – the new Zonar GPS and vehicle information system which can pull up the number and location of each bus in

First operates approximately 60,000 yellow school buses in North America and transports 4 million students every day across the US and Canada.

real time, along with speed, fuel consumption, repair status and inspection compliance.

Every few days a fuel tanker is due in the morning to top up the 10,000-gallon fuel tank – daily consumption is 2,200 gallons.

School finishes are staggered, with children back on the buses by 3.15 p.m. Drivers cannot let younger children off if there is no one to meet them. If a parent is not at the stop then the driver contacts dispatch, who in turn attempt to contact the parent. If contact is not made the driver will return to the stop, and if a parent again is not available the driver continues with the route and returns the child to the terminal.

Older students make their own way home

from drop-off points. Most drivers are back in the terminal by 5.30 p.m., although those on after-school activities runs may not return until 7.00 p.m. Over the day the drivers and vehicles will have travelled up to 150 miles – but for most the drives will have been shorter, perhaps as little as 20 miles.

Before the drivers sign off for the night, they complete a post-trip inspection on the bus and report any defects they have identified. They also have one more vital role. They must check that the bus is empty and display a sign in the back window recording no sleeping children are on the bus. This is the final check of the day; it is done at the end of each journey, ensuring no exhausted

youngster is left on an empty vehicle (soon this will be replaced by a $10m electronic child checkmate across the fleet). The Cincinnati location currently uses the child checkmate system.

With the buses back, the technicians have free rein. Two came on duty before dawn to make sure the buses were all on the road on time, and as the 169-strong fleet roll in they are prepared for the next trip. Each bus gets a full service every 4,000 miles or every 120 calendar days, whichever is the sooner. The later technician shift is the last off-site, at 6.30 p.m., locking the gates behind them after making certain that the fleet is ready for the next morning's runs.

school bus market is currently outsourced and the so-called baby boom echo means it is growing organically by 4 per cent a year.'

Ryder and Laidlaw, the US's biggest school bus provider, had started out in the yellow school bus business at about the same time in the mid 1980s and they grew at about the same rate until the early 1990s, when Laidlaw bought two large regional contractors and raced ahead.

The news of First's acquisition came as a bombshell to Ryder's staff. Carey Paster was then vice-president operations at Ryder. The night before the management team was informed that the division had been sold, he had been in the Town Hall at Pine Bush, New York, guaranteeing officials there that Ryder would never be selling the company off, so certain was he. Hours later he was back there apologising. Paster had joined Ryder in 1986 when his family's 700-strong school bus business was sold to the American company. As part of the deal he agreed to stay on for one year. Thirteen years later he was still there when the company was sold to First. Today Carey is CEO and President, Sales, Marketing and Commercial Development at FirstGroup America and up until 2008 he and Mike Murray were in charge of First's 60,000 school bus operation across North America. 'We were shocked and amazed at the sale,' he said. 'We knew we were the shining diamond in the Ryder portfolio. But we were intrigued to have been sold to a UK company with no school experience.'

He recalls his first meeting with Lockhead and Tony Osbaldiston, who asked

Carey Paster, who has spent his career in the school bus industry.

On rural routes yellow buses may travel a long way between houses.

The use of the STOP sign on buses is a simple but effective device to warn motorists that children may be crossing.

him to go with them to St Louis for eight weeks while they studied the options for the company. Looking back on those early days, Paster recalls how exhilarating it was to be joining a group where they were told to be looking for growth. 'Go out and double the size of the company in five years,' Lockhead told them – a message that was frequently repeated to investors too. Ryder had been a good company to work for, but it was not hungry for growth in the way First was and decision-taking took a little longer, recalled Paster.

Persuading Ryder to sell turned out to be just the first of the British company's problems, though. The new First Student company operated in some thirty-five different states, each with its own legislation, bureaucracies, customs and practices – not to mention the way company operations were run in each corner of America.

As one First US manager at the time explained, there was a 'laid back' approach in the west, a 'conservative' approach in the mid west and an 'aggressive, European style' on the east coast. And then there was the language problem of 'two nations divided by a common language' – as George Bernard Shaw once commented. For a lot of issues it was a minor inconvenience, although on fairly fundamental subjects for a transport operator. Many parts of a vehicle, for example, have a totally different name. For 'boot' read 'trunk', for 'bonnet' read 'hood', and for 'windscreen' read 'windshield'. Even fuel has a different name, petrol being called 'gas'.

Of more concern were different definitions for the same word. A worker in the UK would be pleased to hear a manager talking about a pension scheme. But in the United States an employee would recoil in shock as 'scheme' equals 'scam' in American parlance.

Another cultural difference between the two continents was the tendency in America to accentuate the positive and make little of the negative – an admirable quality for much of the business, but with First's obsession with budgetary control it soon caused problems.

Earlier, when First had started looking to expand its empire abroad, there were two possible targets in mind in the United States, and each had their champions within the company. Both were transport operations, but to Lockhead and the advisers around him there was one market that looked the better bet. The other business was Coach USA, a coaching to tourist bus operation which later suffered badly when people stopped travelling around the time of the first Gulf War. In the end it was bought by another British transport operator which was later forced to dispose of some of the company during the economic downturn.

While the internal Ryder v. Coach USA debate was under way, a third opportunity appeared on the company radar screens, and this deal was completed just days before Ryder. The company was Bruce Transportation, founded ten years earlier in New England by Bruce Lyskawa with a fleet of twelve buses. His goal had been to grow the company to five hundred buses in ten years and then sell it. He was spot on with the ten years, but he had been so successful that he had accumulated a fleet of 1,200 buses, nearly two and a half times as many as his original goal by the time he agreed to sell to First.

Quoted after the two purchases, Moir Lockhead said: 'A quarter of our income now comes from overseas – and we could double that in the States alone over the next five years. The US passenger transport market is worth $25 billion a year with the yellow school bus market accounting for $14 billion.'

As part of the deal with Ryder, First bought two other key businesses: in public transit contracting, soon to be called First Transit; and fleet maintenance services, which became First Services. Both play an important role in First's success. In the beginning there were concerns that First Services would not fit with First's core competences in running buses. Osbaldiston remembered that at the time the company felt: 'It is easy to say "This is not core, let's get rid of it!" But if it looks good, we have to ask the question "Can we make it work?"

Some First Student fleets have to cope with considerable temperature variation. This snow-covered fleet is in picturesque Sedona in Arizona, a state more noted for its heat.

First companies are keen to see new environmentally-friendly technologies coming into service.

If it doesn't work out, and you decide that it's not where you want to be, at least you are selling a going concern.' Those debates did take place in First until the new companies proved themselves and the skills they brought with them added to First's core competences.

The key time in the school bus calendar is from mid January through to April, when the bidding round takes place right across North America. Each state has its own rules, but in general school bus contracts run for between three and five years and school board officials look for a balance of the best fixed price and quality to meet their needs.

For First and other operators it is a time of both risk and opportunity. Every five years or at a shorter interval, 100 per cent of the company's school bus contracts are renewed or lost in these bidding rounds. Often up to seven different companies bid for each contract. Competition is fierce and there is a raft of unknowns – a major factor is who can best guess fuel prices, pay rates and insurance over five (or fewer) years. While First does not want to lose a contract, understandably it has no wish to operate a contract losing money.

At the same time other companies' businesses are exposed when their contracts come up for renewal. Across the nation First Student has bid development teams scouring public announcements for contracts going out to tender. First has always had a number of advantages when it comes to these bidding rounds. One is its size, which can deliver economies of scale. For example over the five years to 2012 it will be buying 25,000 yellow school buses – more than the entire bus fleet for many countries. That generates huge discounts and also allows the company to get vehicles developed to its own specifications.

It can also buy fuel at bulk discounts and hedge the price, thereby minimising the risk of future price hikes. The company's size means it can fling resources at an operation that might not be operating at 100 per cent too. Most importantly for the client, though, the company culture, training, safety standards and customer-focused service mean that most customers want to renew with First once they can agree terms.

As a result, amazingly, up to 99 per cent of contracts are renewed each year despite the intense competition from other companies. Further, with Laidlaw operations now part of First, the company routinely expects to win contracts for up to 2,000 extra buses each year either from competitors or from newly privatised services like those of Mr Rawis, the superintendent in Pointe Coupee, who earlier highlighted the problems parishes like his faced.

He recorded what happened:

A solution was sought to provide service under the same state and federal guidelines for transportation, but at a reduced cost. Enter First Student, and what a relief! As Superintendent of the Pointe Coupee Parish School Board, I was pleased to find that this nationwide school transportation company exists, and that they provide turn-key service equal to, if not better, and at a far lesser cost.

This sort of organic growth is much more cost effective than the company's acquisition programme, whereby it goes out and buys in-fill acquisitions or strategic purchases to take it into a new part of North America. It wins growth without having to buy the company.

First Services

One of the smallest, newest and most geographically spread parts of FirstGroup is the US-based First Services. It was born out of the acquisition of the Ryder school bus business back in 1999, which brought with it a small municipal vehicle maintenance business looking after anything from local-authority lawn mowers to fire engines. In First terms it was small beer and it was known at the start as First Vehicle Services. First did not even know whether it wanted to keep it.

But back in the UK at the start of the new millennium First began to take a look at the whole facilities management business. It had noticed that companies were increasingly starting to focus on their core business and contracting out the routine chores like maintenance to other companies that specialised in them. Facilities management companies would be invited to bid for the maintenance contract for a whole company from managing the estate, maintenance of buildings, vehicles and equipment, and so on. When companies saw what a burden they were relieved of, along with the operational and cost benefits that came with it, they started to look to other areas they could outsource. Their contractor would happily take on the work. There were clearly good commercial opportunities here.

First realised it had a lot of the core skills associated with facilities management – such as flexible management, running and maintaining large vehicle fleets, cost control, partnerships with the public sector, central purchasing, and so on. A business with no major capital or acquisition costs was also appealing and First believed that with a shake-up and the help of a couple of small acquisitions it could compete with the best.

Everton Bryan was brought in to head the new operation. Given the range of work it planned to get involved in, the company's name had to change from First Vehicle Services to simple First Services. Before leaving in 2008 Bryan transformed what was a $60 million turnover business that was not going anywhere into a $250 million turnover company which, in the space of just five years, now competes for businesses alongside global giants like Halliburton. The company is now also the largest private-sector provider of customised on-site vehicle maintenance and ancillary services in the US, while staff numbers have grown from nine hundred to around three thousand to service the growing client base.

Today while First Services customers are entirely US based, their operations on behalf of US government clients are far more international than any other part of First. They range across Spain, Italy, the Virgin Islands, Guam and even Diego Garcia – a small island in the Indian Ocean that can only be reached by flying to Singapore and then boarding a US military jet aircraft to the island.

First's work at these exotic locations is part of the company's contracts with both the US Air Force and US Navy, with which it has a series of key contracts across the nation and overseas. In the industry these contracts are known as 'base operational support'. Bryan likened the role to maintaining a small town. On Diego Garcia, for example, the military are dependent on First for their

These pictures illustrate the range of work First Services teams carry out in support of US industry and the military, leaving them able to focus on their core skills.

daily water and power needs in the community, with First Services teams maintaining both the island's power plant and water treatment plant. The assets are federally owned but are maintained by First. Other contracts include fleet maintenance, warehousing, IT support and security.

Elsewhere in the public sector, First Services has targeted police forces and the maintenance of their fleets. By the nature of their work police cars come in for some punishing treatment – with multiple drivers, high-speed driving and even damage by offenders they are chasing. Police chiefs need to have confidence that their fleets will be fully operational whatever the punishment they have received.

The early contracts with police fleets were begun by the old First Services Ltd, but the revamped company recognised the advantages it could offer police chiefs, and today the company maintains nearly seventy police fleets around the United States, including a flagship contract in the nation's capital, keeping the police cruisers in the Washington DC force out on the streets fighting crime.

Contracts guarantee the serviceability of up to 96 per cent of the fleet at any time and commit to having police cruisers back in action within hours of their entering a maintenance depot. The police vehicles themselves are just part of the equation. Each one costs the taxpayer about $23,000, but that is half the cost of the in-service vehicle with all the electronic equipment necessary for police work which can be supplied and fitted by First.

Fitting rugged, reliable computers for police fleets soon became a First speciality, and today they slide into special rugged metal docks manufactured to First's specifications in China. First's expertise in this area has brought a range of other customers, particularly in the utilities field. Their on-board electronics equipment means employees out in the field do not need to return to base to update records, invoices, stock levels and client data.

The efficiency of First's services is praised by its customers. In Fort Wayne, Indiana, the city's director of fleet management recorded: 'Our partnership with FVS is a cohesive "one-team" effort, yielding cost savings as well as industry-standard certifications. Our fleet has grown 17 per cent, but our overall maintenance costs are 15 per cent less than in 1996. We average 99 per cent overall vehicle availability.' To get that sort of satisfaction ratings the company looks for and recruits the best staff in their field and keeps them trained and qualified to the highest national guidelines.

The company boasts that its fleet practices and fleet management have

A day in the life of a First Services company – maintaining Washington DC's police cruisers

At the entrance to the government facility on the outskirts of Washington DC, an armed guard looks up from his desk and opens the gate to admit the first member of staff of the day at the police maintenance facility. It is just 5 a.m. Security is tight; there is one way in and one way out and it is manned round the clock.

Inside, the First Services team keeps the US capital's police force on the move, maintaining a fleet of nearly 1,700 police vehicles. They have to have 90 per cent of marked police cruisers fit for duty every day and 94 per cent of the entire fleet – which includes unmarked cars, stake-out vehicles,

motorcycles, command wagons, bomb trucks, K9 (canine) vehicles and prisoner transports.

But if those targets look tough, First Services had its contract renewed in 2008 and signed up to some jaw-dropping targets – 96 per cent all-time availability for the entire fleet and 93 per cent for the police cruisers. To deliver targets like these the First team has to operate two shifts a day and if they cannot complete the backlog by Friday night they come in on Saturday too – not that that is often necessary.

The 5 a.m. arrivals at the depot are the service writers who in the next few minutes will

start receiving the first of the daily flood of marked police cruisers. This fleet takes a hammering. The vehicles are on duty twenty-four hours a day, manned by three separate crews whose lives may depend on them. To ensure reliability, each vehicle is called in for a full service every three months or every 3,000 miles – whichever is the sooner. Across the nation First now maintains police vehicle fleets like these for some seventy forces.

The service writers log the details and requirements for each of the arriving Ford Crown Victorias, the famed US police workhorses, and the worksheet is time stamped and a copy given to the police driver

First maintains this elite police fleet which protects the US President and America's capital city.
TOP RIGHT: A Washington DC police cruiser maintained by First. This fleet operate twenty-four hours a day. As each police shift ends, they hand over the car to the next officers on duty.

before the car is allocated to a work bay. By 6 a.m., when all the sixteen vehicle bays will be staffed with First technicians, a stream of thirty or so of the 5-litre police cruisers will have arrived for their routine service. Each will be back in service later the same day, complete with another time-stamped document recording how long it spent out of service.

Over on the motorcycle bays those of the force's 55 massive Harley-Davidson motorbikes or 120 smaller police bikes due in will have arrived. Meanwhile the new vehicle technician has started fitting the flashing lights and horns on a vehicle fresh in from the manufacturer.

At 10 a.m. work stops and the technicians are called in to one of two daily safety briefings – one for each shift. Safety is paramount across the group – the team is updated on new initiatives, safety statistics and incidents elsewhere and given lessons that can be learned from them. All forty of the staff will be attending daily briefings, from the General Manager through to the operations manager, stores team and technicians.

By the time the briefing is over, the first of the daily trickle of vehicles needing urgent attention to stay on the road are being brought in. Problems range from a routine mechanical or electrical failure to a flat tyre. Any failure is

one fewer police vehicle on patrol and all must be dealt with while the crews wait.

First was contracted to run the fleet soon after the start of the new millennium. The police chief had brought in another outside contractor because of a huge backlog of unfit vehicles, but things did not work out and First was selected for the job. Today there is no backlog and First sticks to its targets.

The staff are proud of what they do. These are some of the highest-profile vehicles in the land. The Harley-Davidsons are called in to form the convoy outriders when the US President is travelling in the city and to give protection for other visiting heads of state and their convoys. The police cruisers have to be a credit to the nation's capital, where security is of utmost importance. And undercover police must know they can depend on their stake-out and shadow fleets.

At 2.30 p.m. it is time for the dawn shift to head off home and the evening crew to report

for duty. Meanwhile the accident co-ordinator is checking with the bodyshops. First subcontracts to ensure vehicles damaged in car accidents are being repaired and will be back in the depot. Elsewhere in the depot, stores clerks are making sure the spare parts inventory is on target.

Up to eight times a year the First team have to be extra vigilant. The police chief may be holding one of his regular crime purges, the World Bank may be meeting or the capital preparing for 4 July celebrations. For each occasion the capital demands that every vehicle possible is available for duty and First technicians put in extra hours to ensure that happens.

Now, though, it is 11 p.m. and the last of the technicians are signing out for the night. The parking lot is empty, ready for the morning arrivals and for the process to begin all over again. Across the city the vehicles that were in care today are back on duty.

offered customers considerable savings. Typically, it says, its customers save an average of 17 per cent a year on their fleet maintenance costs by using First technicians. They also get an improvement of up to 10 per cent in vehicle reliability.

First Transit

Back in the 1980s when Margaret Thatcher and the government were deciding the fate of the UK's municipally owned bus companies, Ronald Reagan was in the White House thinking similar thoughts about America's publicly run bus operations.

While Thatcher grasped the nettle and legislated for bus operations to be set up as stand-alone companies and sold off lock, stock and barrel to the private sector, Reagan hedged his bets. Instead, he settled for a mandate requiring 25 per cent of services to be outsourced to the private sector.

Meanwhile, in Cincinnati, a company called ATE Management & Services Inc., founded in 1955, was developed to exploit these new American opportunities and provide the management support and expertise for privatised operations. Among the staff was a young law clerk called Mike Murray who is today President & CEO Operations for a fleet consisting of around 120,000 vehicles,

Mike Murray, President & CEO Operations, FirstGroup America.

First's North American offices in Cincinnati, Ohio.

including First Student US, First Transit and First Services. ATE was able to offer anything from consultancy advice through to the operation of complete mass transit operations on behalf of public-sector clients.

In those early days the hope was that the efficiencies of newly outsourced operations would lead to demands for local authorities to outsource more mass transit responsibilities. It never happened. However, the outsourcing process has not continued at the speed the private sector would have liked.

ATE, a Ryder Public Transportation Services Company, soon expanded and fed off the opportunities that outsourcing presented, it caught the eye of the Ryder school bus operation and was soon snapped up, only to become part of a new division of FirstGroup when Lockhead bought Ryder's yellow school bus operations in 1999.

First found a transit company that operated on low profit margins, suffered major accident claims, and was at the margins of First's then core business. It watched as other UK companies with similar operations in the US pulled out of the sector. Meanwhile the US executive team came up with a number of options for the business which resulted in Murray being put in charge and tasked to turn around the business.

At its low point First Transit was operating 115 contracts in twenty-six states. They ranged from consultancy advice to the management of city transit services through to the delivery of bus operations themselves. But while some local authorities would threaten the public sector with further outsourcing if they pursued excessive demands for pay hikes, overall there was little extra movement to the private sector.

First Transit services in North America.

Murray and the team decided to refocus operations, boosting safety, moving into new sectors and submitting more realistic tenders. The operation of para-transit (on-demand services for people with disabilities), transport call centres and shuttle bus services became new targets.

Today the company manages and operates in some 250 systems in forty-two states, Canada and Puerto Rico for transit authorities, state departments of transportation, federal agencies, municipal organisations and private companies. It is the market leader and largest transit bus contractor in the United States and the largest airport shuttle operator, and it has transformed safety under First's corporate culture. Injuries involving lost working time fell 70 per cent in a single year, traffic collisions fell by more than 15 per cent in three years, and injuries involving staff dropped 33 per cent. The company has downsized its fixed route operations from 80 per cent of the business to 36 per cent and grown the para-transit operations to 38 per cent and shuttle services to 14 per cent. Call centres make up the rest of the business.

The company operates public transport systems on behalf of transit authorities in cities such as Los Angeles, Houston and Denver, and carries 125 million passengers a year. Altogether the division manages some 20,000 staff – 13,000 of them First's own employees and the rest under the company's management. First Transit is the largest provider of airport shuttle bus services in the US, serving airports in cities such as Baltimore, Philadelphia, Houston and Miami.

One of the sectors that First Transit has focused on in recent years is call centres for para-transit services, linking people with disabilities with vehicles to take them to their chosen destinations at a time that suits them. The largest is in New York, where some 500 staff were working in their then Manhattan offices when a plane ploughed into the World Trade Center in September 2001. The staff were evacuated into the street, in the shadow of the two towers, and watched in horror as the second plane crashed into the other tower. But they regrouped and within a few days were operating normally from a temporary location. It was a tribute to their determination that they were able to swing back into action so quickly.

There is no end to the range of services that the company has turned its hand to – from ferrying prisoners around New York to providing shuttle buses at an old people's campus in Florida. In New York State First Transit operates the range of motor coaches that transport caged prisoners around the state accompanied by armed deputies riding shotgun. It is a business the company

If this looks like a big fleet of yellow buses, set it in the context of the 60,000 buses First Student operate across the United States and Canada.

would like to expand to other parts of the country. In Florida, the home of many retirement communities, the company provides shuttle buses for a campus of 20,000 elderly people, transporting them to facilities such as shops, cinemas and medical centres across the community area.

First in Canada

First did not wait long after buying into America to make a move north of the border into Canada. There, in 2000, just a year after moving into North America, First bought Canada's third largest yellow bus operator, the Hertz Bus Company. Its fleet of 735 buses criss-crossed the prairies and wheatlands of the province of Saskatchewan, which boasts cities with names like Saskatoon, Moose Jaw and Swift Current.

By 2004 the group had moved into British Columbia, buying up the nearly fifty-year-old Farwest Group, for which revenue grew 59 per cent in the four

years after the group bought the company. It now operates a 356-strong fleet with more than six hundred staff. In 2005 First looked to Calgary, Alberta, for another acquisition – the then 58-year-old Cardinal Coach Lines. It bought a controlling interest in the company, which operates 1,500 school routes daily.

Laidlaw

First had stalked Laidlaw for years, but it was never the right moment. The directors either would not deal or the company was in Chapter 11 bankruptcy – in the US Chapter 11 allows a troubled business to file with a federal bankruptcy court for protection – saddled with the debts from its medical operations and waste disposal business (Safety Kleen). It was not until 2007 that First could finally strike.

Laidlaw's fortunes had ebbed and flowed. Founded by Robert Laidlaw in Windsor, Ontario, in 1924, the company started out as a trucking business. It really took off in the late 1970s – it entered the school bus business in Canada in 1979 and the US four years later. The bus business had become so successful by 1984 that the company left the trucking business altogether to focus on the schools market.

Laidlaw continued to buy up hundreds of small school bus and transit businesses across North America, becoming the largest provider across the continent and operating some 40,000 buses. But then they did what First had never done: they branched out into non-core activities. In the medical services industry they bought American Medical Response, an ambulance service provider, and Care-Line Inc., a company that consolidated smaller ambulance businesses.

But its big acquisition came in 1998 with the $403 million purchase of Greyhound, which had been crippled by a drivers' strike in 1984. Another strike by drivers in 1990 helped take Greyhound into bankruptcy and, although it later emerged from that, the impact of 9/11 on domestic travel kept Greyhound in the red. Laidlaw itself, burdened by problems with the medical businesses, filed for Chapter 11 bankruptcy in June 2001 and did not emerge until June 2003.

Nonetheless, by the time Laidlaw was sold to First it had an annual revenue of $3.2 billion and pre-tax profits of $498 million. It brought with it 62,500 staff, 40,000 yellow school buses, transit vehicles, 2,350 Greyhound buses and 26 per cent of the outsourced yellow school bus market.

It created an energised First that is now so big that the superlatives trip off the tongue. It is the largest public transport operator in North America. It is by far the largest yellow school bus operator in North America – more than three times larger than its nearest competitor. It is the largest private-sector provider of transit management in North America and the largest private-sector provider of vehicle maintenance services on the continent.

Success in the school bus market does not come by standing still. Each school board has to retender services every few years and there is fierce competition for the work. Schools, parents, pupils and school boards all need to be confident in the services being provided and regular checks are made to ensure the vehicles are 100 per cent safe.

Investment and innovation keep First Student's operations out in front. In the last six years the combined company has invested $540 million in new yellow bus fleets. As the manufacturers' biggest customer First can expect priority, competitive prices, quality service and vehicles tailored to the company's needs. Safety is of paramount importance to the company's operations and First Student's standards always exceed the programmes and practices laid down at state level. Each year $4 million is invested in driver training, with every single driver going through annual safety and security training.

With a customer satisfaction rating of 96 per cent and a contract retention rate in the 90s, First is repaying confidence in its services by introducing two new technological improvements. The first is Zonar, a nationwide computerised safety, security and productivity system. The second is a new GPS service for each bus, allowing the dispatcher to know precisely where each vehicle is at any time.

The Laidlaw acquisition was a classic case of Lockhead playing the long game. Soon after First had moved into the US school bus market, Laidlaw saw that the company was going to be a far more aggressive competitor than Ryder had been and invited Lockhead to New York to see if there was any chance of doing a deal with them. To Lockhead there were similarities with the Badgerline deal but, this time, with a premium to Laidlaw shareholders.

But any deal was too soon after the Ryder purchase for First, and Laidlaw was not prepared to strip out its loss-making medical businesses. Later Laidlaw was to change its Chief Executive. Lockhead kept his ear to the ground and crawled over any news he could get on Laidlaw to give himself an edge in any future negotiations.

Some of the North American yellow school bus fleet.

Meanwhile First's US management team from Alaska to Boston were complaining about Laidlaw's aggressive behaviour towards First when the British company won business off them. Lockhead flew to Chicago to meet Laidlaw's new Chief Executive, Kevin Benson, an ex-airlines manager. The two got on well together but Benson made it clear that he had a big job in getting out of Chapter 11 and growing his business.

The two tried to keep in touch, but nothing moved forward until Connex moved into the US transit market, buying a business run by a much smaller British company, National Express. Benson believed there was an opportunity for First and Laidlaw to put their transit businesses together. The two companies signed a confidentiality agreement to see what might come out of it. They then started to talk about a broader joint venture, but each time Greyhound was a stumbling block.

Finally the two sides saw the prospect of a deal and a memorandum was put together for it. Later Lockhead was surprised to see that, under tough US legislation, Kevin Benson had recorded all his conversations with the English businessman and included transcripts in the memorandum.

Greyhound

One of the newest parts of the First network needs little introduction to anyone anywhere across the western world. Almost everyone is familiar with the Greyhound long-distance coach network even if they have never visited North America. It is one of the great American icons, along with Coca-Cola and the yellow school bus.

Founded in 1914, it now carries 24 million passengers a year on 2,350 buses to 3,100 different destinations. There is scarcely a corner of the United States and Canada from Alaska to the Mexican border and the Pacific to the Atlantic that isn't served. Routes even link into Mexico through subsidiary companies and partners. Greyhound became part of First when its owner, Laidlaw, was bought by FirstGroup in 2007.

Like the airlines, it operates through a system of hub and spoke services which allow passengers to travel across the continent from small town to small town with minimal delay and just one change at a major city hub.

Until it was overtaken by domestic aviation, it had replaced the stagecoach and railroad as the way to cross America by public transport. During the

David Leach, President, Greyhound.

A Greyhound 'Silversides' service travels down the west coast of the United States. Before the spread of the plane, a Greyhound service was the way to cross America. The name 'Silversides' refers to the GMC model PD3751 bus used by Greyhound (and others) from the late 1940s until the early 1960s.

The Greyhound brand is recognised all over the world.

Second World War US servicemen used its services to criss-cross the continent to take up new postings, and new settlers to North America made their way west aboard company vehicles. Even today the network maintains its links with the national rail network Amtrak, which will sell tickets to any town in the US – the parts not on the rail network being connected by a Greyhound link.

Today you can buy a ticket to take you more than 2,800 miles across North America for just $99 (£50). Services operate around the clock with rest stops every three to four hours. All services have restrooms on board and night-time vehicles have reclining seats and reduced lighting. A month-long Greyhound pass will give you the freedom of the continent for around £260. Generations of backpackers have taken advantage of these passes to explore the continent, sleeping on the overnight services to save their spending money.

Just looking at Greyhound's average journey times for its really long haul services gives a feel for the vastness of the continent it serves: San Francisco to Detroit, 58 hours; Dallas to Washington DC, 32 hours; Los Angeles to Miami, 62 hours; and Los Angeles to Montreal, 72 hours.

The logistics of running an operation across these distances is almost incredible – for example some 60 per cent of drivers have to stay away overnight as part of their normal work pattern, often using driver hostels set up for the purpose at Greyhound terminals, and the company has thirteen maintenance depots around the country. Although Greyhound is famed for its passenger services, it also uses its network to provide an express next-day parcel service across the continent.

Laidlaw bought Greyhound in 1998 for $403 million when it was still struggling to recover from a crippling drivers' strike in 1984. Curiously, First had been pursuing Greyhound at around the same time – but, as so often, was not prepared to pay nearly as much as the winning bidder. Another strike by drivers in 1990 helped take Greyhound into bankruptcy and, although it later emerged from that, the impact of 9/11 on domestic travel kept Greyhound in the red.

Over the years Greyhound has been through numerous management initiatives, but until Laidlaw many did not address some of the fundamental issues like loss-making routes. Nonetheless First inherited a company with a few other issues that played to the company's core strengths. It had retained enormous overheads which First could quickly reduce.

David Leeder, the then First main board director working closely with Greyhound, remembers how he found many cities where Greyhound had cavernous bus stations and ticket offices totally inappropriate to either today's operations or customers' needs. That needed to be changed fast. Astonishingly, he identified that it was not possible to reserve a seat in advance – so passengers ran the risk of showing up on time, not being able to board a full bus and having to wait perhaps twenty-four hours for the next one. That is being addressed.

A Greyhound service in Long Beach, California. Twenty-four million passengers board a Greyhound bus every year.

The first of Greyhound's new BoltBus services offers a new style of service for passengers, providing direct express services between key eastern seaboard destinations and airports.

Leeder and Dean Finch, the new First Chief Operating Officer for North America, found that Greyhound's Dallas headquarters had more finance and IT staff than the entire FirstGroup headquarters in Aberdeen. They were housed in two eleven-storey downtown office blocks along with the company call centre. First, with its focus on front-line rather than back-office staff, could soon see economies which could instead be invested in the fleet.

First also has the talent to boost revenues. They found that Greyhound had been a seasonal business and there were whole market areas and customers that were not being exploited. Success depended on major changes to operational efficiency, perceptions, investment and marketing. In particular they needed to sharpen up service delivery and on-time performance.

No new Greyhound coach had been ordered for nearly five years when First arrived on the scene. Within days First had placed an order for fifty vehicles for the launch of their innovative new BoltBus service. They have already rolled off the production lines and been brought into service – a big morale booster for the staff and an encouragement to customers. They have been introduced in a brand-new type of service to link New York to key eastern seaboard destinations and airports by express services, cutting out many of the intermediate halts and using downtown pick-up points more relevant to today's traveller. This offers broader appeal to commuters and students, and early bookings have already been promising.

One of the problems with all public transport is filling empty seats, particularly in quiet seasons. At the moment some 85 per cent of Greyhound travellers book for their journey only three days before they travel. The average journey is just 450 miles, most being in the north-east corridor. One of the most popular of all has been the journey linking New York to the Atlantic City, New Jersey, casinos – where vehicles regularly run full.

New internet and ticket-pricing initiatives aim to change the way people travel and book. Pricing incentives will encourage people to travel off peak and in different seasons, and to use Greyhound as an alternative to other forms of travel.

Both Leeder and Finch are convinced that Greyhound can rise up and become the proud transport icon it once was.

A two-way trade?

Having taken up yellow school bus operations in the United States, First recognised almost immediately that the system could solve a lot of transport problems in the UK too. The US National Safety Council has found that yellow school buses are 172 times safer than a car and eight times safer than passenger trains. The company felt it was pushing at an open door when it brought a right-hand drive demonstration bus over to the UK in 2000.

As part of the Yellow School Bus Commission's review of home to school transport, a modified school bus toured Britain gathering the views of the general public, including thousands of children.

It was welcomed with open arms everywhere it went. Local authorities, MPs and schools themselves asked if First could give them a demonstration. All were worried about child safety, the age and condition of traditional old UK school buses, discipline on board, traffic congestion, the school-run scrum around the school gates and cost.

With up to 20 per cent of traffic on UK roads at the morning peak being on the school run, the yellow school bus and its near door-to-door pick-up system being the safest form of transport anywhere on the roads, and the company agreeing to provide brand-new vehicles for all contracts, the choice looked like a no-brainer.

At presentations First managers stressed that the bus itself was just one part of a safety-conscious network that involved a partnership between parents, schools and operator. Drivers were in radio contact with their operations rooms, were on the same bus every day, knew the children by name and would not tolerate bad behaviour. Children were picked up at or near their homes and given safety training at the start of every year. Drivers would often be mothers at the school served by the bus.

The bus turned heads everywhere it went; the media lapped it up and demonstrations were always well attended. At council presentations there was

The first of the UK fleet report for duty. The lights above the windscreen, an important safety feature in the US, cannot be used in the UK as regulations do not allow them.

often a full turnout by councillors who at the end would ask enthusiastically 'What's the next step?'

There was just one place where there was a stunning silence: the Department of the Environment, Transport and the Regions. Officials at this mammoth government department had recently developed a school transport policy which just scratched at the surface of the problem – focusing on cycling to school and walking buses, both worthy initiatives but hardly likely to bring about a fundamental shift in behaviour. Government officials – who turned out to be at odds with their own ministers – lined up to highlight obstacles to First's proposals. One even told a First manager that it would come into service in the UK over his dead body, such was the animosity.

Success in the UK market, First believed, depended on two things: being able to use the iconic yellow school bus vehicle recognised by children the world over and being able to import new vehicles at a similar price to those in the US. First even held preliminary talks with manufacturers to see if the vehicles could be assembled in the UK if demand took off. The civil servants' main objections were to be vehicle construction and use regulations and disability legislation. First appealed to the department to see if it could bring together officials from all the different government departments involved to work together with First to see how any difficulties could be overcome. That never happened.

The disability officials in the department insisted that every bus had to be low floor and accessible to disabled children. First pointed out that the seating area was deliberately set up high so that in the event of any accident the point of impact would be well below where the children were sitting. The whole idea was to stop casualties and prevent students becoming disabled in the first place.

Inevitably vehicles for disabled people were much more expensive to manufacture since they had to be fitted with lifts, so across the United States only those vehicles necessary for routes with disabled children would have one. Since the bus company knew which child was on which route every day it was easy to ensure those routes were served by a special lift-equipped yellow bus.

The department insisted on nearly fifty design changes before they would allow a yellow school bus to carry children on UK roads – despite the fact that 470,000 of them were in operation in the US and that they had been developed to federal guidelines and had been in service for nearly eighty years. The net result was that

Some of the few yellow school bus services in the UK.

a bus that cost around $35,000 in the US would cost more than $140,000 in the UK. And since brand-new yellow school buses would have to compete for local-authority school bus contracts against near life-expired 25-year-old double-deckers, the US style service would not be able to compete on price.

Eventually First appealed to ministers and a meeting was held in a House of Commons meeting room with a junior minister and an enormous support team of civil servants from across the department. Official after official lined up to highlight the difficulties of proceeding with the project. Not one ventured to offer a solution. Finally First appealed to John Prescott, the then Secretary of State for the Department, and to David Blunkett, then Education Secretary, whose own officials were much more supportive. They both jumped at the idea and insisted on launching it jointly at a Scottish Labour Party conference in Glasgow.

On 17 February 2001 Prescott told the media: 'I am pleased we are now able to give the go ahead for the pilot schemes using American-style yellow school buses ... I hope they will be a success with more and more parents feeling this is a good option for getting their children to school safe and sound.'

The key words here were 'pilot schemes'. With the officials who loathed the whole idea controlling the pilots it was no surprise to First when there was no national roll-out later on. The wishes of politicians, parents, schools and operators lost out to the intransigence of the civil service. Exactly a week before Prescott had defied his officials, they had launched their own guide to encouraging children to go to school by bus. The yellow school bus was not featured.

Despite the attitude of officials, work continued to get yellow school buses on UK roads. Twenty vehicles were shipped over from the US and some local authorities were persuaded to sign contracts. Nearly nine years on, there has still been no national roll-out of yellow school buses. First still operates a limited number of schemes within the bureaucratic straightjacket civil servants have created.

Hope is at hand. FirstGroup established and sponsored a commission headed by former Education Secretary David Blunkett to look at the whole issue of home-to-school transport which reported favourably in September 2008. The all-party group examined and quantified the potential benefits of dedicated home-to-school transport and reviewed the yellow school bus model. It concluded that their widespread use across the UK would benefit the economy, the environment and the general health of the nation.

The Yellow School Bus Commission headed by former UK Education Secretary David Blunkett (centre) which was set up to look at home to school transport.

The revolutionary new **ftr** service seen outside York Minster.

York was the first city to introduce an **ftr** fleet.

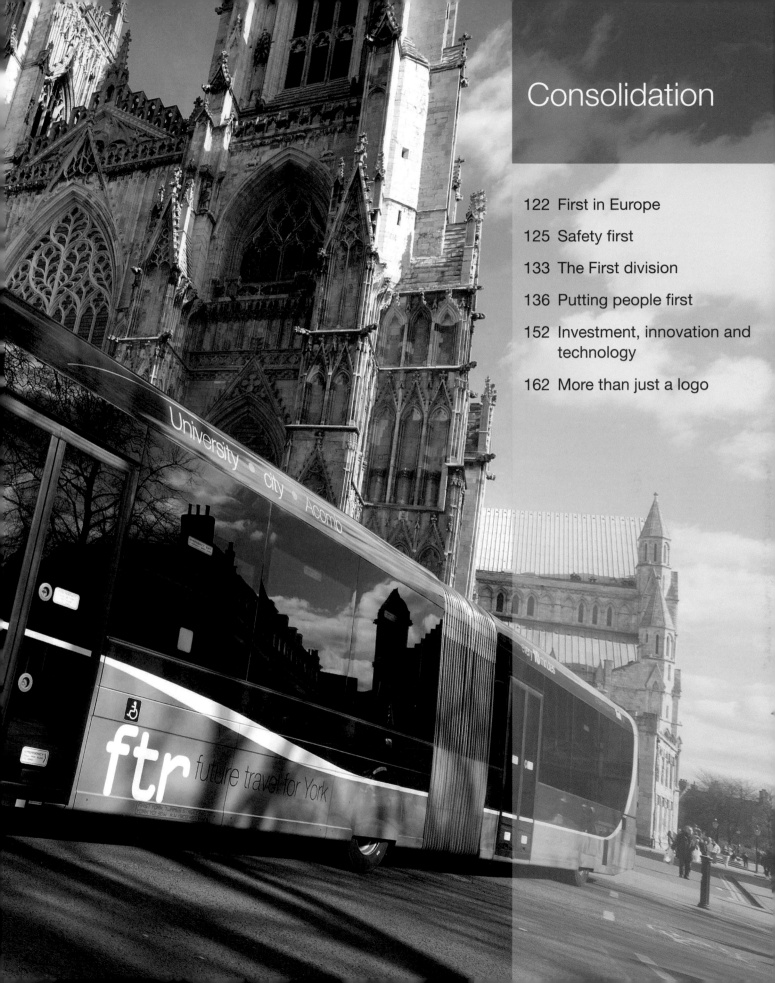

Consolidation

First in Europe

First took a long time to dip its toe into continental Europe – opportunities there just did not fit its acquisition or risk profile. The continent was way behind the UK in transport privatisation, the regulatory risk was greater and the margins were lower. Today, though, the company is running transport operations in four countries: Denmark, Sweden, Germany and Ireland.

First off the ground was a small, privately owned company in Dublin which provided a luxury coach link between Dublin Airport and the city. Established in 1999, today the fleet is nearly sixty strong and runs luxury leather-seated coaches between the airport and Dublin, Cork and Belfast as well as the car-park shuttle service at both Belfast's George Best Airport and Dublin Airport. Under First the business has almost doubled in size and its operations on key Dublin routes run twenty-four hours a day with passengers able to check live on-line exactly where each vehicle is.

Germany saw First's next acquisition. In 2007 the company bought three family bus businesses run by Arthur Merl in Mannheim, Ludwigshafen and Heidelberg. The 200 staff and 130 buses run city and regional networks along with school and worker transport. The country looked a good bet. Its 80 million population has a tradition of using public transport – twice as much as in the UK in fact. But while it is opening up all parts of the transport market, the pace of change has been slow. The structure of the market is much more complex than in the UK, and by value the biggest part by far is rail, where the privatisation process started with the franchising of single branch lines to test the market and delivery.

Cathedral Square in the historic Rhineland city of Speyer, the home of the Arthur Merl business.

The Merl vehicles have been rebranded in First livery.

First is a partner in the operation that runs trains linking Denmark and Sweden.

However, there are also big municipal transport networks, some of them operating their own tram and metro networks, and the core bus businesses run by hundreds of small companies. First's acquisition allows it to dip its toe in the market and test the potential for future growth. It has also been busy introducing First's culture, standards and values to the new business and has started to make small in-fill acquisitions.

Further north, First has entered the market in a rather different way by forging an alliance with DSB, the Danish railway operator, taking a 25 per cent stake in a new contract that started at the beginning of 2009, running fast train services linking Sweden and Denmark across the longest combined road and rail bridge in Europe at Oresund.

The famous Oresund Bridge links Denmark with Sweden.

Nearly 10 million rail passengers crossed the sound in 2007 using a modern fleet of eight-coach trains on routes that start at Elsinore (the home of Hamlet's castle) and pass through Copenhagen, the city's airport – and on over the bridge into Sweden where the line divides, going both to Malmo and Gothenburg. On some stretches of the route trains are running every ten minutes. Once the trains arrive in Sweden they fan out on lines up to 100 miles from Malmo.

En route the traffic crosses the world's longest border point and switches from one type of signalling and electrification to another in mid bridge.

Safety first

Safety and customer service are at the heart of everything that First does, wherever it operates. The company is obsessed by these core values, which give a lead to other UK transport operators. And there are good reasons why.

Since rail privatisation there have been three tragic rail accidents on the Great Western railway. None was FirstGroup's fault, but each sent shock waves through the company. On 19 September 1997 a Great Western high-speed train ploughed into a freight train near Southall, killing 6 people and injuring 150.

A First Great Western Adelante train at the approach to Paddington station.

The driver had gone through a red light, an inquiry found. First did not buy the company until the following year but inherited its responsibilities in court. The driver was initially charged with manslaughter but the case was dropped. But Great Western Trains was fined £1.5 million for not having a warning system in operation on a long high-speed journey.

On 5 October 1999, just two years after Southall, a First Great Western train was involved in another tragedy a few miles away, at Ladbroke Grove just outside Paddington Station. A Thames Trains service leaving Paddington drove through a red signal and crashed nearly head-on into the path of an incoming First train which had a green light for its track. A total of 31 people – including Brian Cooper, the First Great Western driver – were killed and 227 people were admitted to hospital. A further 296 people were treated at the site of the crash for minor injuries.

First Great Western had previously complained to Railtrack, the then infrastructure provider, about the dangers of this set of signals. The later public inquiry found that Railtrack had not taken appropriate action despite eight trains having passed the same signal at red in the previous six years.

Then in November 2004 at Ufton Nervet, Berkshire, a chef committed suicide by parking his car on an unmanned level-crossing in the path of a Paddington–Plymouth express. Train driver Stanley Martin had no chance of stopping in

Sir Moir Lockhead officially opens First Capital Connect's Performance and Training Academy and Simulator Centre, a £1.2m state-of-the-art investment that is used to teach new drivers and helps support and develop existing drivers.

time and he died with five of his passengers. An inquest jury decided the chef had committed suicide and unlawfully killed the six victims who died with him.

Although nothing could remotely compare with the pain and suffering of the victims and their families, these experiences were devastating for staff too. To go through just one of them would be traumatic enough for any company, but some managers had to deal with all three.

First had already decided before Ladbroke Grove that it would do everything in its power to ensure that if ever there was another rail accident it would not be because of anything the company had left undone. At Southall the Automatic Train Protection (ATP) system had not been working. It was a trial system, it was not mandatory and it had been pioneered by British Rail. It had never worked properly, being a marriage of new technology and old rolling stock, and it had been retro-fitted to the trains and track. If working 100 per cent of the time, it would physically stop a high-speed train from passing a red signal and it could have prevented the Southall accident. By the time of Ladbroke Grove, First's engineers had boosted performance from 20 per cent to 80 per cent reliability, but the extra 20 per cent proved elusive. Since First's train was running

All staff have a copy of the Injury Prevention handbook that is helping in the fight to reduce accidents and injuries to staff and passengers.

Company engineers now routinely follow the safety rules, which insist on high visibility jackets, hard hats and protective glasses in workshop areas.

legitimately on its track at Ladbroke Grove, it would have taken an ATP system on the Thames train to have prevented the disaster – and there wasn't one.

Lockhead decided that in future his trains fitted with ATP would not run if the system was not operating properly – even if it meant cancelling trains. He banged heads together and found that the root factor was a reliable supply of spare parts for failing systems. Within weeks the manufacturers had made them available and to this day the 100 per cent rule applies for all First high-speed services where there is the ground infrastructure to support it.

While First's managers, safety teams and engineers had a clear idea of how they could keep their network as physically safe as money, manpower and technology allowed, the board believed it was time to get some independent help. And as an Aberdeen-based company it knew exactly where to turn for it – to Du Pont, the company which had helped transform oil rig safety after the *Piper Alpha* explosion and fire in the North Sea that killed 167 men in 1988. Originally explosives manufacturers, they had pioneered workplace safety initiatives since the early 1800s.

They did a complete safety audit of First's operations, proposed new working practices and helped institute a new total safety culture. They taught First that incidents can lead to accidents, which can lead to injuries, which can lead to fatalities. You therefore need to go back to the root cause and stop the incidents.

At the top First introduced safety as a permanent feature of every single plc board meeting. Each month the board was required to know about safety trends, incidents and progress on new safety initiatives. Between meetings board members had to be individually notified immediately by e-mail of every single serious safety incident. The Chief Executive has to be updated by phone on each one.

Before the company's executive monthly management board meetings attended by the top executives from across the group, an hour-long executive safety committee meeting is held which probes incidents and safety practices, challenges statistics and introduces new practices. For example in 2007, following a report by the government's Transport Road Research Laboratory, there was a decision to ban the use of all mobile phones by all company staff when driving a vehicle on company duty – whether or not they were hands free. (Bus and train drivers had always been subject to such a ban.)

To gain maximum benefit from these meetings, outside experts from the Health and Safety Executive and other parts of the industry, along with non-

A First ScotRail train is dwarfed by the stunning Scottish landscape.

As well as boosting revenue, ticket barriers have helped in the fight against anti-social behaviour and crime. Now that vandals have to pay for a ticket before they can scrawl graffiti in train carriages, they have found other targets.

In the struggle to protect customers from terrorist attacks, armed police sometimes have to be deployed at major stations.

executive board members, are invited to attend. Outside the meetings directors are expected to carry out safety tours of the company sites they visit. These visits will include checking that workshop staff know safe working procedures, finding out when they were last tested and seeing that staff wear their high-visibility jackets and are up to date with company programmes.

On the ground every single activity the company carries out has to be safety audited before being introduced, and every passenger-carrying route is inspected. For example on a bus route there are checks to see whether bus stops are located away from corners or blind spots and to make sure that there are not any overhanging trees that could cause a problem.

Some of the issues and some of the solutions are simple, but the consequences can be far reaching. In the US one of the problems for the whole industry was children falling asleep unnoticed at the back of a yellow school bus. First's solution was simple: to instruct each driver to walk through to the back of their vehicle every night and leave a sign on the back window saying 'Bus empty'. There can be no second chance for staff who leave a child on board.

This obsessive attention to detail has rubbed off on staff, and there are many stories of the team reporting behavioural change outside work – for example using safety glasses for DIY projects and refusing to use a hands-free phone even when driving their private cars.

More importantly, since First introduced its Injury Prevention initiative with its accompanying slogan 'If you cannot do it safely, don't do it', statistics have shown the impact of what is being done. During 2007 alone for example, injuries involving the loss of working time across the group fell by a staggering 27 per cent from what had been a fairly traditional base. Even that overall success is outclassed by some remarkable divisional achievements. Rail injury figures plunged 60 per cent and First Transit in the US was close behind at 58 per cent. First believes that once timeless initiatives like this deliver cultural change, the benefits can last forever.

Within the UK Bus division the company Safety Council sets safety targets and ensures adoption of best practice. Central to that is the reduction of passenger injury and vehicle collision rates. Drivers are trained to ensure they practise safe driving and are equipped to manage situations that may be beyond their control. New driver training standards have been introduced across the UK Bus division. These incorporate continual professional development to meet the requirements of European legislation, which calls for all new bus drivers to hold a certificate of professional competence.

As well as introducing a defensive driving programme, the company has been evaluating new driver camera technology in London and York. Forward- and back-facing lenses trigger a camera to record events such as sharp braking. This information can be used to review driver behaviour and help learning, and can capture useful information during collisions. The London trials have contributed to a 90 per cent reduction in unsafe driving behaviour and a 25 per cent reduction in collisions.

What no one chooses to highlight within the company – quite deliberately, because it would appear callous and was not the reason for doing it – is that a major focus on safety makes good business sense too. Fewer accidents mean fewer claims, cheaper insurance, fewer days lost to injury and fewer out-of-service vehicles or repairs.

Both rail and bus driver training simulators have entered service – First Great Western alone has three. These realistically simulate the view from the cab and the movement of the train. They also allow drivers to practise reacting safely to incidents that could not be attempted on the track – for example a brick dropped from a bridge smashing a cab window.

Safety initiatives have mushroomed across the group over the years, and the company has monitored what has been happening elsewhere, borrowing new ideas that might have a relevance to First's front-line staff. One initiative borrowed from the airline industry was for conflict-avoidance training for front-line staff. If signals fail and trains run late, it is frightening for members of staff to be alone on a platform trying to help customers in circumstances where they are likely to be verbally or even physically assaulted by an aggressive passenger. Training helps them take the heat out of the situation.

First also works closely with trade unions in trying to design measures to protect staff. Vandals these days are only too aware that if they cause trouble on a bus, the incident is likely to have been caught on CCTV and the company will take the evidence to the police. And if the police do not take action or the courts prove too lenient, then the company is prepared to take civil action against those involved.

Some First initiatives have a double benefit. Gated ticket barriers at platforms fulfil a dual role. They were designed to reduce fare dodging but they have also proved to be a powerful tool against vandalism. It was fun for vandals to ride trains and scrawl graffiti when they could dodge paying, but having to buy a ticket as well soon cut numbers of offences right down. Over the years many other initiatives have been introduced to reduce vandalism. The old First Great Eastern franchise used to play classical music on some station platforms. Vandals could not stand it. CCTV cameras at stations have expanded rapidly and have played a major role in reducing crime.

The most expensive deterrent of all to vandalism – but an essential one – has been to replace broken or scratched windows and paint over graffiti immediately. Once vandals get to know that they and others are not going to have a chance to look at their handiwork, it stops being so much fun. This quick removal of damage creates a less threatening travelling environment, albeit at a cost of several million pounds per year.

In recent years the threat of terrorist bombings and suicide attacks has brought new problems to the public transport industry. First has brought in extra staff and initiatives to minimise the threat and is in regular contact with the security forces about how to protect customers and staff.

Putting safety at the heart of everything the company does has become embedded in the company's actions in a way that goes far beyond handbooks and slogans. It has now become so automatic that at all levels of the company it spills over into the way they think and behave outside work, from driving to DIY.

The First division

If Moir Lockhead has been the inspiration and driving force for the growth of First, the company's success has been delivered by an extremely young and talented management team and staff on both sides of the Atlantic. Many have climbed quickly up the ladder on the back of early successes with the group. A classic case is Dean Finch, who was still in his 20s when, as a chartered accountant working for KPMG, he was brought in to help bid for rail franchises. He threw himself into the work, helping to develop a company foothold in the new market.

Of the first five bids just one was successful – for Great Eastern, which was later to become both an operational and financial triumph for First. The other four franchise victors might have put in a more attractive initial offer to the government, but they were not a financial success and none of them survived on the original terms their owners had negotiated.

Soon after First was created by the merger of Badgerline and GRT, the company had the chance to acquire the remaining 75 per cent of Great Western Holdings, which by then ran both North Western Trains and Great Western. So much of his time was then being spent on First business that Finch was poached by the company to become commercial director of its rail businesses at the age of 30. By 2001 he had been appointed Managing Director of the company's Rail division. Finch looks back fondly at that time as among the most challenging and enjoyable experiences of his career.

It was a gruelling seven-day-a-week job driving up basic operational performance and standards during a period when Railtrack, the infrastructure provider, let down the industry with its nationwide speed restrictions after gauge corner cracking was found at the site of the GNER rail accident at Hatfield in Hertfordshire. Great Western was to be a test bed for Finch's ideas to boost performance, motivate staff and provide customer service.

His achievements were hailed by the then Secretary of State for Transport, Alistair Darling, as delivering the fastest improving railway business in the industry. Along the way he had introduced NVQs for staff, giving them and the company the skills that the group really needed. He brought in a new customer service directorate with real resources and teeth. Those teeth were in the shape of a compliance team that made very sure that the standards the company was setting were both achieved and maintained.

Former director David Leeder is regarded as one of the great brains of the transport industry. During his seven years at First he was managing director of UK Bus, and more recently was a key player in turning around Greyhound.

It was during Finch's time with the Rail division that the company explored and delivered extra seats and services, bringing real economic benefits to towns and cities along the inter-city routes. Passengers along some of these found that instead of a high-speed train to London every couple of hours they were getting three to four an hour. And Oxford suddenly saw that instead of the commuter trains it was used to, it was starting to get 125 mph trains, some with catering.

Finch turned the rail companies around financially too so that by the time First was looking to beef up its financial team and was looking for a new finance director for the group, he was the natural choice. He was then 36 and faced a daunting challenge.

The company had been a victim of the dotcom boom (and later bust) that saw money pour out of good solid businesses like First into pie-in-the-sky businesses that existed only in people's dreams. There were real question marks in the City about First's future. The rail businesses accounted for around a third of the company's turnover, yet all the franchises were coming to an end by 2006 and there was no guarantee of any continuity of earnings.

Nick Chevis and Nicola Shaw.

During Finch's reign as FD oil had started at $28 a barrel, only to soar to near $100, costing the group some £50 million, the equivalent of nearly 40 per cent of profits. Meanwhile the post-dotcom shares collapse left the group (like many other companies) with a pensions' deficit of some £300 million. Impressively the board decided not to let staff down (as many companies did at the time) by introducing money purchase pensions, but to give the much greater commitment of career average pensions – a position that was to cost the company over time £250 million which Finch had to find. By 2007 the fund was in surplus again.

One way of getting new confidence back in the City was to secure the Rail division's future, so Finch took overall control of the rail bidding round for the second generation of rail franchises. Faced with the daunting prospect of a rail business without any rail passenger franchises, he helped win franchise after franchise and took the group to the position of largest rail operator in the UK with a secure revenue stream for the next ten years – all at a time when other companies still had to defend many of their operations in the new bidding round. Better still, each new First franchise quickly started delivering passenger and revenue growth.

The company's reputation in the City was restored and the £2.50 share price

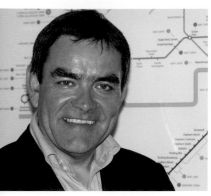

Two of the current non-executive directors, Audrey Baxter and David Begg.

that Finch had started with had tripled to £7.50 by the time he moved on to his new job as Chief Operating Officer in North America, running a business with a turnover bigger than the entire operations of most UK transport companies.

The board had sent Finch to America in 2007 to oversee the acquisition of Laidlaw and to merge its operations with those of the existing First businesses in the US. At the time he started, the company still had to complete its US anti-trust clearances – a task that took six months, over two million pages of documents to the Department of Justice and bilateral meetings with the attorney generals in each US state that had issues with the acquisition. And that was before the staff from two rival companies could be welded into one seamless team of 99,000 people. Finch and the deal were not popular with all Laidlaw staff. In Laidlaw's Chicago headquarters Finch's office was next to the men's washrooms. He went in one day to find six bullet casings lined up facing him on a washbasin. When the police were called they suggested it was a warning signal to Finch that he was going to be 'closed down'.

Back in Aberdeen Finch left behind him his young deputy, Nick Chevis, as the new acting Finance Director, a man who was in the financial hot seat when the share price rose up to over £8 before the subprime and credit crises bit deep. He was a man with a ready smile but was ruthless at stripping out unnecessary costs and at finding commercial opportunities and exploiting them.

Other key figures on the UK executive management board had also risen young to the company's key posts. Nicola Shaw, the Managing Director of the UK Bus division, is the only woman at such a senior level in the UK public transport industry and she took up the role at the age of 36. She has brought a structure and discipline to the division at a crucial time for the industry.

Many other companies would dearly love to have a management team of this quality, experience and youth backed by the maturity and experience of directors like Lockhead and Barrie. It is a sign of how the transport sector has changed since the early days of privatisation. But there is strength in depth on both sides of the Atlantic too – backed by impressive management development programmes and the knowledge that any manager who proves themselves can be quickly propelled into bigger and more high-profile roles.

Watching over this executive team are the non-executive directors on the main board chaired by 52-year-old Martin Gilbert, the Chief Executive of Aberdeen Asset Management, a company now managing £100 billion of third-party assets from offices around the world. Gilbert has been on the board from the day GRT was privatised; his company was one of the financial backers of the fledgling business back in 1989.

Talent has not just gone one way, though. First's top people have been highly valued across the industry. Three examples make the point. Dr Mike Mitchell, First's UK Chief Operating Officer, was poached by the government to head up the Department for Transport's rail operations. Peter Hendy, who was running the UK Bus division when he left, was picked by Ken Livingstone to be the Transport Commissioner for London. Meanwhile Clive Burrows, probably the most respected engineer in public transport, was chosen by the government to become the rail industry technical director; his work included specifying the technical requirements for the next generation of high-speed trains.

Putting people first

Workers in the UK transport sector and those aspiring to join it since the wave of privatisations in the 1980s have not always been well served by the country's training and education system. The UK government abandoned the nation's apprenticeship programme which had served so many craftsmen so well in the past. Then there was the education system's continuing failure to turn out school leavers with the basic skills of reading, writing and arithmetic. These and the normal social skills of being able to relate to customers were sadly lacking from many applicants for jobs with the company.

The *Sunday Times* reported in 2007 that five million UK working adults lacked functional literacy, while seventeen million had difficulty with numbers – something of a handicap for a potential bus driver collecting fares!

To start with transport employers, including GRT and later First, did not help. Buying public transport businesses meant borrowing money and delivering the cost reductions, efficiencies and revenue growth to pay off loans. Back-office jobs that were not perceived to be contributing to revenue growth were stripped out to help each company meet its targets. By 1999 there was just one First bus company with a human resources manager – and that was London with its traditional trade union challenges.

First companies paid the price in terms of high staff turnover, the interface with customers and performance. The problems were not just with staff but

The architects of First's Rail division success –
Moir Lockhead and, left, Dean Finch.

with managers too. There, the situation was different. There just were not enough high-quality managers in an industry that had traditionally been used to managing decline.

Entrepreneurial skills, quality control and attention to detail along with the drive and enthusiasm associated with the private sector were not always there in sufficient strength. The big transport operators had not yet had the time to develop home-grown talent, so they poached each other's. Several things came together at around the same time to turn the tide. They included branding to create a new national image, falling unemployment which created staff shortages, and operational weaknesses with some services unable to run because there were not the crews to operate them.

By the late 1990s First had started rolling out its new corporate brand. If it was to mean anything it needed to be backed up by good performance and good, customer-focused staff. Falling unemployment in economic hotspots and a variety of local employers all chasing the few people available for hire put that at risk. They might not be suitable applicants, and with an industry average of 30 per cent staff turnover per year companies could soon reach crisis point with staff shortages and cancelled services.

First had recognised that there was little point in reinventing the wheel at every local company. Until then each First company had its own local way of advertising for and recruiting staff, of training them and using them, and their own terms and conditions and benefits.

Pay could not be the only solution to more and better staff – bus operators had not only to compete with many other employers in the labour market; they had a customer base which was resistant to the fare increases that would be necessary to cover the cost of pay rises. New ways had to be found to make working life more attractive and to encourage people to stay.

First's research showed a range of reasons why First had high staff turnover and why performance was suffering. Driving a bus with its anti-social hours and customer interface was not always a popular choice when someone could work 9 a.m. to 5 p.m. for the same money driving a white van with no passengers to carry or fares to collect. As a result there was not a lot of choice in who the company took on, and new drivers often left soon after training. Some that stayed found it difficult to relate to customers, and embarrassments like a man with a guide dog being turned off a bus because the driver was allergic to dogs and an elderly woman falling over because the driver pulled away from

Due to new **FirstGroup** initiatives staff turnover has reduced.

the kerb before she was seated damaged both the relationship with customers and the brand.

Meanwhile unemployment continued to fall and First could not always find replacements. Job shortages meant some bus services had to be cancelled, which meant unhappy customers, a worsening reputation, a Traffic Commissioner who threatened the company for service failures and lost revenue. This was a crisis that needed to be dealt with quickly. Across the industry driver turnover was running at 30 per cent and, with each driver costing £3,500 to train, the company needed to find the right staff.

Actions were quickly put in place. Managers not known in an area went

through the driver training programme and reported back on what it must have been like for a new recruit. They found that new drivers sometimes felt unsupported, that junior managers could be harsh and that they had not appreciated how lonely it could be out on the job.

The company determined that there was no point in recruiting someone if they were not likely to stay or if they were not going to get on with the customers. Real attempts needed to be made to boost starter pay rates, provide a friendlier working environment and provide more support for new drivers. As new initiatives were working through, the company decided to accelerate vacancy filling with the recruitment of Polish drivers. At the worst of the crisis there were nearly a thousand driver vacancies around the UK. But the Poles

First took buses to Poland so the company's Eastern European recruits could familiarise themselves with the vehicles before they left home.

came – and they stayed, taking the heat off the problem and buying time for the new initiatives to bed in.

Changes in the companies were radical. Some of the fundamentals of the bus industry were shaken up. At the interview stage managers started to make clear what a potential driver would be facing: early starts, late finishes and sometimes threats by young passengers. What was the point of new recruits only finding out once they were out on the street?

New recruits had an experienced driver nominated as a buddy who would stay with the new driver long after training had finished and the driver had entered service. Rosters were made more user friendly to account for changing working patterns outside the industry. If someone wanted to work only early or late shifts, why not? In some depots crèches were introduced to encourage mothers of young children to come back to work.

Managers were told to listen more to what their staff had to say (and to act on it) and to give them regular appraisals. Staff facilities and canteens were improved and employees were consulted on new uniforms and afterwards given a choice of which items they would prefer to wear.

The company beefed up safety initiatives to protect staff and customers with measures such as security screens and CCTV cameras on board buses. Vandals on the buses were given notice that the company would take out private prosecutions if the police would not act. Saliva kits were provided so staff could collect offending spit for use in evidence in court. In Scotland youths who

Practical experience for new drivers.

New staff must have language, customer service and safety skills before joining First companies in the UK.

vandalised the fleet were warned that civil action would be taken against them and the courts would order them to repay the company when they reached adulthood.

But it was the longer-term cultural changes that had so much impact. If pay could only rise in line with jobs of similar skills, then there were plenty of other things the company could do. Some, of course, had already been introduced early on when GRT was privatised; others had been started informally with trade unions – the Transport and General Workers Union (T&G) has part-nered many initiatives with First. However, it has only been in the years since 2000 that the groundbreaking initiatives have shown real fruit or taken on a cross-company hold. Some started as part of an organised programme, but others arose because a local manager had taken the initiative.

Historically most transport workers remained in relatively low-skilled jobs for much of their working lives. Progressively First has offered them an alter-native – a second chance to improve their education and basic skills, and to boost their working opportunities to allow them to reach their full potential. A classic example was workplace learning centres. In Basildon in Essex Chris McCormick, who had started life as a bus driver and had been promoted to run the depot at Basildon, saw staff who had not excelled at school but clearly had more to offer if given the chance.

He got together with the local Learning and Skills Council and the T&G union and developed plans to open up an on-site learning centre for staff to use between shifts. Typically, when Moir Lockhead got to hear about it he offered strong support and came to visit.

The results were staggering. At the outset staff used their spare time to paint and equip an old office in the depot. Computers were supplied and courses discussed and agreed. Favourites were holiday Spanish and computer basics. Outside lecturers came to help. Quickly the facilities became oversubscribed. One of the most powerful sights was the depot award ceremonies where out-siders like the local MP came in to present certificates to successful staff. To watch the pride on employees' faces as they came forward to accept awards for classwork for perhaps the first time in their lives was very moving.

There were other surprises too. Depot morale perked up and even staff who would never have volunteered for anything were seen studying in their time off. Families were allowed to come and share the facilities too. Lockhead quickly saw the potential for rolling the scheme out and recognised the importance of the partnership with the T&G. It was their conveners rather than local managers who encouraged staff to make use of the facilities.

Today there are more than forty company Workplace Learning Centres in First companies across the UK, including mobile bus-based classrooms for smaller depots. More than 60 per cent of staff have access to the centres – there are plans for 80 per cent access – and they are backed by a hundred trade union learner representatives. More than 4,000 staff have already achieved road passenger transport vocational qualifications as a result.

One of the staff to study at a centre was Gail Gisby, who joined the company as a bus driver before being promoted to a driving instructor. She explained: 'I decided to use a learning centre to improve my maths and English. When I left school I had few qualifications and in my new job as a driver I had to deal with money and the public. My problem was not adding up fares, it was working out the change afterwards.'

Another advocate was Carl Newman, who did not do well at school because of undiagnosed learning difficulties. His local First workplace learning centre recognised his needs and catered for them. The result: he passed adult literacy and numeracy tests and won First's Lifelong Learning of the Year Award.

The company's apprenticeship schemes have started delivering results too,

Joe Mackie, one of the original members of the 1980s buyout team, receives an award from the Princess Royal at First's Aberdeen dinner and dance in 2007.

Sir Moir Lockhead likes, wherever possible, to hand out awards to apprentices, management trainees and workplace learning students to show the importance the company attaches to them.

Chris McCormick, right, presents another skills award. McCormick has pioneered First's skills training, setting up the first company Workplace Learning Centre and then rolling them out around the UK. His work has won praise from Government ministers.

with an award ceremony held in 2007 to mark the end of the first four-year programme – the first of what is becoming an annual event. With the programme expanding to 135 engineering apprentices in training, the first awards were to six bus engineers successfully completing their training. For David Pick from South Wales, who was honoured for being the best apprentice, the benefits were clear. 'First could not have been more supportive,' he said at the time. 'The company has financed and guided me each step of the way. Having now qualified, I am keen to progress as far as I can with First.'

Training and development for staff and managers has proved not only good for those involved but for the company too. When these programmes started First was haemorrhaging UK bus drivers at the industry average of 30 per cent a year. That figure has been cut to 22 per cent and saved the company £2.8 million in lost management and recruitment time and driver training. And the company is pushing to improve this figure still more.

A 2005 GoSkills statistics report showed that only 2 per cent of staff in the transport sector received any leadership training. First took this as a challenge and set up its Learning and Development Ladders based on workplace learning and mentoring. By the end of 2007 the early results of its First Into Management programme to help move staff from the shop floor onto the first rungs of management showed around six hundred supervisors holding Level 2 NVQs in team building. As managers advanced they had the opportunity to join the Leadership Horizons programme, which has more than a thousand graduates across the group. These graduates with high potential are given the opportunity to apply for programmes to achieve the Institute of Directors' Certificate in Company Direction before moving on to the MD development programme for potential managing directors.

Dave Kaye, COO of First UK Bus, said: 'No other transport company offers this level of qualification to their employees.'

Each year the company also takes in graduate trainees on a partnership programme with the Open University Business School and the Chartered Institute of Logistics and Transport. The first of its kind in the UK, the programme contains both academic and transport themes and works towards an MBA. And beyond that the company has programmes of formal mentoring for directors and issues-based coaching.

Industry magazine *RouteOne* has said First's 'approach, scale and level of commitment is unique. Training and development does not stop, either because

Lockhead in the driving seat of a First train. Behind him is Dave Kaye who was at the time managing director of the First North Western franchise and is now chief operating officer for First UK Bus.

you reach a certain age or level in your career and neither does it ignore middle or senior managers.'

First's initiatives soon came to the attention of central government: ministers trumpeted First as an example of what the private sector is capable of in areas as diverse as workplace learning, lifelong learning, recruitment and on-the-job training. Company managers are members of government working groups guiding the country on what works best for industry. Managers take to the conference platforms to show other employers what can be achieved.

In the UK Rail division the company progressively opened training academies for its staff, providing onward support for new recruits for anything from customer service training backed by NVQ-level certificates through to complete driver training programmes. Front-line staff are also offered confrontation avoidance training, helping them to lower the temperature if customers become aggressive. At the driver training centres new recruits train on realistic train simulators that resemble their future train cabs and can simulate eventualities that are too dangerous to practise out on the track.

Across the Atlantic, as well as their induction training, yellow school bus drivers get a day's additional safety training each year and the company has been actively looking at how it can develop UK-style practices in the very different workplace of North America.

Early familiarisation with the company's uniforms.

Staff are proud of their smart uniforms – which they helped choose.

First likes to make sure that the effort which staff and managers put into their training is recognised, with staff being very publicly congratulated for their initiative. At the company's annual dinner and dance in Aberdeen, for example, managers who have just successfully completed a course are brought centre stage to receive their certificates from Lockhead.

When looking at relations between staff and the management of FirstGroup, one needs to set the two in the context of the times, if only because it makes what has been achieved more remarkable. The public sector, particularly its transport element, has traditionally been a bastion of the trade union movement, and a particularly militant element at that. On the other hand, the early bus barons were regarded as a rather brutal form of capitalism.

In the public sector, British Rail was known for the willingness of its trade unions to strike to get their way. The publicly owned bus sector was grossly overstaffed and, like the railways, riddled with so-called Spanish practices. Even today 90 per cent of First's UK workforce are members of a trade union, and in the United States the figure is 40 per cent.

Curiously, in the early days of UK privatisation there were not the huge clashes between the two sides that some had predicted. On the railways that was partly because the unions had to get used to negotiating with twenty-five different train operating companies rather than one large and soft bureaucracy, but also because their front-line train drivers happened to do rather well from privatisation. On the bus side staff cuts hit the less militant back-office staff rather than the front-line drivers, who would all still be needed. Private-sector owners were only too well aware of the damage a crippling strike could inflict and both sides had a common interest in wanting their sector to grow and prosper.

First had started out as a particularly staff-friendly company – not least because it was, unusually, a management and staff buyout. Staff shared in the rewards of success and also in the management of the business and pension schemes through its employee directors. As it grew bigger and bought up other companies, it had to try to assimilate the different company approaches into the First way of doing business.

With his shop-floor background, Lockhead had a natural affinity with the issues his staff faced and wanted to give them the chance to reach their full potential. At the same time, by the mid 1990s the company realised that a happy and stable workforce was as much in their interests as the staff's, so a

Wayne Spence, one of First Great Western's team at Bristol Temple Meads station, was voted Rail Personality of the Year at the National Rail Awards for the cheerful and helpful way he provided information and looked after passengers.

Ipswich based bus driver, Leon Wells, winner of the UK's Best Bus Driver at the Bus Driver of the Year Competition and recognised for exemplary customer service at the UK Bus Awards 2008.

major programme to rationalise and expand opportunities and benefits was put in place. Trade union officials were very active in their development.

One of the most remarkable dimensions of First's staff relations and corporate management is the employee director. The role was there at the birth of GRT in Aberdeen and today it extends to almost all First companies across the UK. Together those employee directors elect one of their number to sit on the group's overarching plc board. That director is the voice of the staff and sits alongside the company's executive and non-executive members at every meeting and strategy session and is present at every outside visit the board makes. The employee director is a central part of the company's decision-taking function.

The main plc board employee director in the six years to 2008 has been Martyn Williams, a revenue inspector at First Cymru, the Swansea bus operator. It is a strange life, dividing his time between checking that buses are on time and tickets correctly sold, and trade union activities and duties with both the plc board and the local company board. Maintaining his 'day job' role, as he puts it, has been important to Williams as it keeps him in touch with staff and issues at local level. Nonetheless it can be a lonely position sitting at the First Cymru board meeting, with local managers only too aware that he knows much more about the FirstGroup parent company than they do.

The role of employee directors has evolved over the years as the company has grown. Curiously, at one time there were trade unions that opposed the concept of First's employee directors. That was based purely on a fear that it would reduce the role and importance of the trade unions in the workforce. In practice the roles are very different and the development gives an extra strength to staff – direct to the boardroom. To this day an employee director on a plc board the size of First is not that common.

When Williams was elected to the plc board, he sat down with Lockhead to learn about his new role and responsibilities, and went on an Institute of Directors' course. The employee director is the staff's representative on the board, but that does not mean going back to the trade unions (or local management) and reporting on everything that has been said and decided. Much of the work takes place outside board meetings. Local employee directors will come to Williams on an issue they cannot resolve with management locally. With his board authority Williams can go straight to the heads of the UK Bus and Rail divisions to seek settlement without even having to raise the matter at a board meeting.

Martyn Williams, the employee director on the plc board.

Williams was surprised at the warmth of the welcome he received on the board from non-executive directors who come from the world of high finance, investment and industry. 'They were a lot more friendly than I expected,' he recalled. His relationship with them has made it easier to raise issues at their level. But do they really have any empathy with the workforce? 'Their hearts are going in the right direction,' said Williams. 'Although they are committed to the shareholder they have the view that a happy workforce is a profitable one.' At first Williams was concerned that there was no human resources director on the main board, but that improved when a new non-executive director started focusing on those issues.

It was interesting to hear first hand Williams' thoughts on how Lockhead's commitment to the staff came through: 'I have been in the board where Moir has stood up and argued the case for employees.' He particularly remembers the way Lockhead fought to keep company pensions at a time when many companies were abandoning them. The employee directors are treated seriously by the executive directors too. At regular employee directors' sessions Lockhead and other top managers report back on what the company is doing and on upcoming issues. Similarly the employee directors are able to raise issues of concern to the staff. Sometimes the employee directors feel they have to go over the head of their local MD to the head of the Bus or Rail division. They always get a sympathetic hearing and often issues can be resolved quietly without any management / trade union confrontation.

There are two sides to First's relationship with trade unions: pay and working conditions, and then everything else. Inevitably the first is of a more adversarial nature and because it is more emotive and the stuff of newspaper headlines, it is the one that most people remember. The much more rewarding and non-confrontational side for both is the partnership in developing safety, training, security, benefits, pensions and savings initiatives. Going right back to the launch of GRT, First staff have been encouraged to take a stake in their company and share in its success. The most recent winners were the 3,000 front-line staff who doubled the value of their investment in just three years, most of them making profits of more than £3,300. Under the company's Save as You Earn scheme they were able to buy shares at a discounted price of £2.67 apiece when the market value was in excess of £6.70.

But just as First has evolved and changed over the years, so has some of the trade union movement. A Work Foundation report in 2005 showed UK union

Ben Fogle, Nell McAndrew, Liz McColgan and Gavin Hastings join Sir Moir Lockhead at the start of the First Monster Challenge 08. The 120 km team relay duathlon around the shores of Loch Ness is organised and managed by First and aims to raise money for charity.

First's human resources specialists donned their overalls and Wellington boots and transformed one of the Cornerstone Project properties in Aberdeen in a team building exercise with a difference.

membership sinking from 13 million in 1979 to 5.5 million in the 1980s and 1990s. The study reported on how the role of unions had changed, from emphasising issues such as productivity and investment to today's family-friendly policies, an ageing workforce and fair pay.

Unfortunately relationships with the transport trade unions are not universally good. In the United States a giant trade union called the SEIU – Service Employees International Union – has been engaging in a massive recruiting programme in recent years, notably among healthcare workers, Walmart staff and security guards. Early in the millennium it felt that yellow school bus drivers offered rich pickings.

Technicians at work.

Traditionally First has felt that it is an individual's right to join a trade union if they want to and any new depot should decide in a secret ballot if it wants to be unionised. The SEIU tried to shortcircuit this; staff reported that they were being picked off in their own homes and elsewhere by SEIU campaigners who wanted them to sign away their right to a secret ballot. Because First resisted these tactics, the SEIU tried to blacken the company's name in both the UK and US – even sending representatives across the Atlantic to the annual meeting in Aberdeen. When these initiatives did not bring early success the union went into partnership with the UK's T&G. More recently it has been the Teamsters Union, led by Jimmy Hoffa, that has been leading the campaigns.

Labour relations, welfare and employment practices are very different in the US, and certainly First found that the approach to trade unions there was not at all similar to the European approach. While First had to remain competitive in a very different marketplace, it wanted to make sure its practices were as compatible with the company's UK standards as possible. At the same time it expects union election campaigns to be fair.

To that end First recruited former trade union shop steward and Labour MP John Lyons to investigate and report back on the allegations being made about the company. His report was circulated to the board and to interested MPs. He routinely visited First sites where union recruitment campaigns were being held and ensured both sides honoured their commitments. In August 2008 he joined FirstGroup as a full-time employee in the role of labour relations director.

In the event of any disagreement First has appointed former US Department of Labor judges Daniel Roketenetz, Richard Mills and Bob Smith to monitor the situation and provide quarterly reports to the plc board. To make absolutely sure fair play has been followed the company has introduced a confidential hotline for employees and appointed Professor William B. Gould IV as Independent Monitor. He is professor of law at the prestigious Stanford Law School in California and a former Chairman of the National Labor Relations Board, a post to which President Clinton appointed him. The professor's role is to investigate any alleged breaches or violation of First's policies, with the group volunteering to take any remedial action found necessary.

First hopes that this rigorous approach will put an end to some of the more aggressive trade union tactics. What became increasingly puzzling to First was that some trade unions were deliberately undermining the company's business and therefore the jobs and savings of their members or potential members – half of First's shareholders are its own staff.

One trade union leafleted customers calling for a boycott of First services, while another actively campaigned against First being awarded a train franchise and started lobbying MPs and the government. The issue related to a global trade union alliance they were trying to forge with an American trade union and was something First's UK staff were not involved in or consulted about. The American trade union involved even commissioned public relations consultants and political lobbyists to campaign against the company and flew UK trade unionists to the US to co-ordinate actions against the company.

The leadership of the T&G was actively involved. It was almost as if the nineteenth-century issues the union described on its website applied today:

The success of British industry in the hundred years from 1780 was built on the exploitation of hundreds of thousands of workers who worked 14 to 18 hours a day for miserable wages in unsafe factories, and lived in bare and comfortless homes. Workers realised they could only fight ruthless employers and inhuman working conditions by banding together, and so trade unions were born – and fiercely opposed by the owners of industry.

As the unions fight to increase their membership numbers, First's US managers are focusing instead on boosting benefits for staff – as far as possible in line with those that staff in the UK receive. Early in the acquisition of Laidlaw, First introduced the same safety culture that had been introduced in the UK, incorporating yellow safety vests and the injury prevention programme. New benefits packages are scheduled to come in too. This is on the back of new apprenticeships for engineers and a graduate training programme. The company has conducted an employee survey of all 99,000 US staff to find out what is most important to them and any concerns they might have.

Though there are no employee directors in the US businesses, the company is piloting an employee involvement committee for its Las Vegas, Nevada, operations. Working within a set of guidelines the committee will decide whether any of the business's policies is being infringed and will have its own disciplinary role for errant staff.

Investment, innovation and technology

First prides itself today on its use of investment, innovation and technology to smooth journeys, make operations more efficient and cost effective and grow the market. Perhaps surprisingly for a transport company, given the public perception of the early days of privatisation, this can be traced right back to the beginning. As the industry faced bus privatisation in the 1980s, services were caught in a vicious circle. The public aspired to car ownership, which meant less money in the fare box, which meant less investment in new vehicles and a consequent further drop in passengers.

From the start Lockhead was determined to turn the tide for GRT. His company would succeed only if it attracted new passengers back to the bus, and that would happen only if journeys were frequent, reliable, comfortable, nearly door-to-door, reasonably priced and able to stand a chance of competing with the car for some journeys.

The age and type of vehicle in service around the UK in the 1980s did not generally offer much hope. With a reputation for being utilitarian and smoke belching, having fogged-up interiors and smoke-filled top decks, they often seemed to be blocking the road with the rear engine access panel open awaiting an engineer. In short, they did not look inviting to potential users.

Worse still, bus routes had changed little for many years. They had not adapted to meet changing demographic and lifestyle patterns. Passengers in a hurry to get from A to B found themselves meandering round C, D, E and F along the way. Journeys were getting slower too as traffic congestion and cars parked at the roadside worsened. If people were going to get stuck in traffic they might as well do it in the comfort of their own cars, as one transport minister observed at the time.

Over the years First developed and fine tuned a range of initiatives designed to win passengers back. While it knew nothing would replace a car parked outside the front door standing ready to whisk a family away in comfort and privacy at a moment's notice for the perceived marginal cost of the fuel it used, a bus might appeal for some journeys or be a substitute for a family's second car. The strategy evolved over the years as the company simplified route structure, made the network instantly understandable to non-users, invested in new fleets, grew to know its markets, offered special promotions and used technology to boost efficiency.

Over the past ten years the company has invested more than £1.2 billion in new buses and trains alone. Many millions more could be added in terms of new technology initiatives and infrastructure projects, both ranging from real-time information to new bus depots and stations.

Most change has been seen on the bus networks, where First has had more freedom to operate, without suffering the constraints of a contractual straight-jacket with central or local government. It is only when one condenses the changes of twenty years into a few sentences that it is possible to see how fundamental the improvements have been and how much further they could have gone if central and local government had played their full part.

A starting point for the journey is the recognition that a bus or train is only one part of someone's journey. To compete with the car First had to analyse the different component parts of the journey and make sure all worked together to create as near seamless a journey as possible.

In brief that meant making sure the bus ran as close to a passenger's home as possible, that passengers could be confident that a bus would be along soon, that the bus stop provided shelter and was well lit and secure, that they knew the bus would go where they wanted, that it would be comfortable and easy to board, that ticketing would be smooth, and that it would take them close to where they wanted to go. It was also important that the bus looked good so people using it did not see themselves as the nation's losers, as Mrs Thatcher once implied they were.

So how did First go about it? It turned out to be an evolutionary process, partly dependent on the business success that allowed the company to invest, the City imperative for more growth, the availability of new types of vehicle and the birth of new technologies that enabled the company to introduce initiatives like smartcard ticketing and real-time information.

Looking back on it, what was remarkable was what little practical help

A bus smartcard – First pioneered their use in Bradford, which had the first city-wide scheme in the UK.

and support there was from central and local government, with some honourable exceptions – particularly given that the bus network was by orders of magnitude the most used form of public transport, the most flexible and low cost and the best-placed weapon to deal with both traffic congestion and social inclusion.

At the outset, what was then GRT quickly started investing in new vehicles – although not at the pace that was to follow. Other things it could do more quickly. Even before privatisation the company had been experimenting with a new form of cashless ticket. Indeed it had reported back in 1989: 'Following a fleet wide trial the company has continued its use of the farecard system which eliminated the requirement for passengers to carry cash by means of a pre-encoded magnetic card ticket.'

From these relatively simple systems the company later moved on to a city-wide smartcard system, this time in Bradford – where the local authority was very supportive. It quickly became popular across the city and First was surprised by its popularity in one quarter, with pensioners. The company had assumed that they would not want to be bothered with new-fangled technology, but instead found that they liked it because they did not have to fiddle with change and did not have to carry it either, reducing the risk of being attacked.

Ken Livingstone, of course, extended smartcard ticketing London-wide and Yorkshire has been creating a county-wide scheme. Expensive initiatives like this depend on public-sector support and, as in so many other public transport areas, it has not been forthcoming.

Bus manufacturers soon started to rise to the challenge of new private-sector markets. One idea that was taken up in Northern Ireland by Wrights of Ballymena among others was the low-floor bus. This opened up new markets to bus companies like First. Young mothers with buggies, people with walking sticks, those in wheelchairs and even mobile elderly people with less flexibility to tackle steps now found that using a bus was no longer an ordeal. William Wright, the company's founder, was the driving force.

The buses were more expensive (sometimes 10% to 20% more) than traditional vehicles but the company saw a demand for them and invested heavily. (Only later did the disability unit at the Department for Transport get involved and introduce the regulations that so curb enthusiasm.)

In 1995 GRT's merger with Badgerline joined up the two companies' experience

Cars and lorries just cannot get along these corridors, which become a clear way for buses.

The little guide wheels (attached to the front wheels of a normal service bus) allow it to drive up these narrow concrete-sided corridors.

Superoute 66, the first guided busway in the UK.

Bus passengers feel very special as they speed past rush-hour traffic stuck on the ordinary roads.

in guided busways – GRT in Ipswich and Badgerline in Leeds. The new FirstBus became the only company in the UK to operate these.

After three years of operation in Leeds, First reported passenger growth of 56 per cent – a phenomenal achievement in an industry so used to falling passenger numbers. 'Of this approximately half, i.e. 28 per cent, has come from people who have transferred from cars. This is made up of both peak-time commuters and shoppers off-peak who now consider the service to be good enough to avoid taking the car into the city centre,' the company reported to the House of Commons Transport Committee.

The concept was simple. Buses were fitted with a small guide wheel at right angles to the main wheel which allowed them to drive down a narrow concrete-sided channel that separated them from congested traffic areas. This channel was only built in places where traffic was traditionally heavy and allowed buses to avoid being stuck in queues such as at roundabouts. Buses then automatically triggered traffic lights to allow them to come out at the head of the queue for the roundabout.

Passengers using the guided bus to get to work could find their journeys up to twenty minutes quicker than by car – the drivers of which watched in frustration as buses sped past them. Another bonus for bus passengers was that their vehicle took them to the heart of the city centre and into gated areas barred to car drivers who had to look for a more remote parking space.

But guided busways were able to work only because of the successful and long-term partnerships and good personal relationships and trust between Passenger Transport Executives (PTEs), local authorities and operators. First contributed to the infrastructure improvement costs and guaranteed the introduction of a brand-new fleet of buses with its own dedicated livery while the public sector put in the guideways and waiting areas.

Sadly the commitment to guideways and taking brave decisions that was shown in Leeds, Bradford and Ipswich has not been so obvious in many other parts of the UK. Success could be easily achieved if operators and local authorities would work together. First could invest all it wanted but, without supporting traffic priority measures, buses would still be caught in the same congestion as everyone else.

Meanwhile the Leeds and Bradford experiences were so successful that since they opened First's Dr Bob Tebb – the company's operations technical manager, who has overseen the guided busway programme – says politicians and bureaucrats from between 150 and 200 countries have seen for themselves why it has been so effective and what it has achieved.

While the towns of the UK are still not covered with guided busways, Tebb reckons the First schemes have had a more hidden but deeply effective impact. They have demonstrated to central and local governments in the UK and overseas an understanding of what can be achieved by segregating bus traffic from other road users. A guided busway is not always necessary to do that.

One of the most radical changes to First's networks of buses around the UK was the introduction of the Overground system, which first appeared in Glasgow in the late 1990s and, after it proved successful there, was rolled out across the UK. It was named as the above-ground equivalent of the Underground map with its award-winning, iconic and easily understood colour-coded network of lines.

Changes to the Glasgow company were fundamental and all had to be in place when the new system was rolled out. The company wanted to make buses simpler to use and the journeys faster and more convenient, and thereby to attract new passengers and make more money for First to enable more investment – a wonderful virtual circle making everyone happy. Before getting there the company had to analyse every route – was it still relevant today (communities do not stand still), could the journeys be speeded up by changing the route, understanding dwell times, what the travel patterns on the route are, are there traffic or infrastructure constraints that could be avoided by changing the route, and how would it fit into a new-look network?

The ftr turns heads wherever it goes.

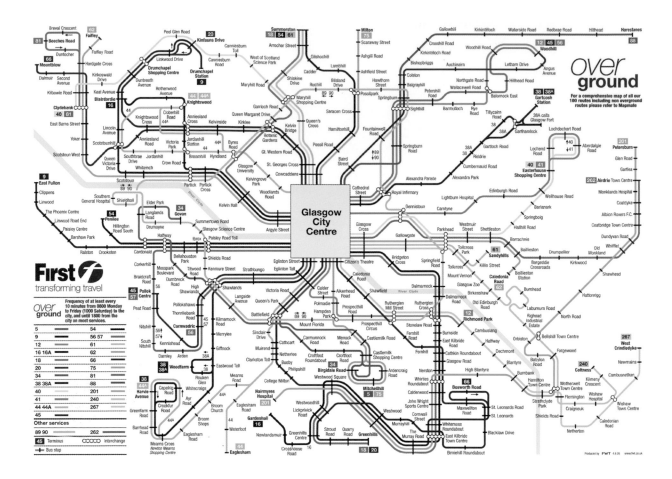

When that was done the company simplified each route by colour coding it as well as providing a route number, and it displayed route details on the side of the bus. Even people not familiar with buses would see that there were routes convenient for them, and with a big investment in new buses they looked good too. To complete the transformation fares were rationalised and communities were sprayed with easy-to-use pocket timetables – although, since the new routes were designed with turn-up-and-go frequencies, they were not necessary for many. Passenger numbers soared and the initiative was rolled out at companies across the UK.

New technology in the shape of mobile phones and GPS quickly found uses in First. Mobile phones allowed customers to text their local bus stop to find out in real time when the next bus would arrive at the local stop. At last passengers could leave home confident that their bus would be arriving at their stop just after they got there. This sort of assurance, time after time, is what is needed to eliminate waiting and encourage passengers to come back to the bus.

Meanwhile GPS technology has been used in any number of ways across First's bus companies. At one level it has been used to analyse individual routes over a week to identify the factors that might be leading to delays – allowing the company to take the evidence to the local authority and work with them to ease problem traffic hotspots.

At another level it helps the company work with local authorities to provide real-time information at bus stops, again giving passengers the confidence of knowing exactly when their bus will show up. The same technology can also be used in company operations rooms, enabling them to chase up late-running buses, stop bunching of vehicles and generally boost services for the passenger.

Technology has also enabled First to overlay its routes in any city on maps, highlighting postcodes most likely to contain potential bus passengers. That enables the company both to target those households and to vary routes if they do not seem to be serving these areas. This work interested the government's social inclusion initiative since it offered the potential to boost services and links for families with no access to a car and created a model which could be adopted elsewhere.

Ticketing for both bus and rail journeys has changed out of all recognition since First started investigating the options. On rail, for example, some First companies are using methods pioneered by low-cost airlines to fill seats at off-peak times. Passengers booking on-line can benefit from variable price ticketing, depending on how early they book before travel. After all, empty seats mean lost revenue that can never be recouped; it is better to have a lower fare than an empty seat.

Fare types have changed too, with period saver tickets offering price reductions and convenience for the passenger and, in the case of buses, shorter journeys for the passenger since most people are no longer queuing on board to buy tickets for every journey.

Perhaps the most exciting piece of innovation has been the development of the **ftr** – short for future – streetcar initiative. Early on in the new millennium First carried out some new passenger research. The company questioned people using new buses branded for a park-and-ride shuttle service. The team was puzzled because the users of the fleet said they never ever got on a bus. Asked

LEFT: Glasgow's Overground map – based on the London Underground concept.

The ftr – an exceptional demonstration of First's commitment to innovation.

how they could say that since they were on a bus at that moment, the passengers replied that they did not regard it as a bus.

This set some in the company thinking. Car users getting on a modern bus for the first time in years are often surprised at how different – and more comfortable – it is compared with the service they used years before, so maybe the outside needed to change radically too. Manufacturers had already made great strides in vehicle design with much greater use of glass for example. Maybe they could go further.

First and bus manufacturers Wrights got together to brainstorm the idea. The conclusion they reached was that a new concept vehicle had to look more like a modern tram – inside and out. Passengers and potential passengers had to think that travelling on one of these vehicles was new and special – a talking point with their friends.

A new design like this, the two companies thought, could appeal to passenger, local authorities and central government alike. At the time light rail projects were running into difficulties. Central government was not happy that costs of schemes in the pipeline were rocketing, that they would have to pick up a lot of the bills and, meanwhile, they would deliver for only very limited parts of the cities where the lines actually ran.

The new **ftr** or streetcar, as it was to be known, offered benefits for everyone. For passengers it offered a futuristic vehicle. For central and local government initiatives would cost a fraction of the price of a tram network, systems would have the flexibility of a bus, no legislation would be needed and major infrastructure developments – disrupting traffic – would be mostly avoided.

The design was crucial and neither First nor Wrights was taking any chances. The whole shape of the vehicles needed to be changed. The sides were given 'skirts' to hide the fact that the vehicle would operate on rubber tyres and the roof was raised to give it a more tramlike appearance. Inside, the driver – to be called a pilot – was given their own separate compartment across the front of the vehicle. Passengers would board behind the wheel arch where there was more access space, and seating design would change so some passengers faced sideways, more like some underground and tram services.

Focus groups were invited to look at and comment on the changing designs, the style of seating, ease of access, comfort and every other factor important to them. Barbara Bedford, running the project for First, shuttled to and from Northern Ireland to make sure their views were taken on board. Engineers came to examine the early prototype to ensure that it would be easy to maintain, cleaners came to see whether it would be practical to look after, and drivers came to see whether it would be a comfortable or easy vehicle to drive. Even the whole plc board came to look at it.

But the vehicle itself was to be just one part of the **ftr** experience. Just as important was where and how it was to be operated. If it was to succeed it had to run on key roads in the cities it served and there had to be priority measures to ensure the vehicle did not get stuck in traffic. People waiting at vehicle stops had to be protected from the elements and given the latest ticketing and passenger information technology.

Finally, the first scheme was ready. York, with its commitment to public transport, wanted to be first and was prepared to provide the priority measures and infrastructure support the scheme needed. Like any new technology and system it had its teething problems, but today they have been overcome and the scheme is being looked at enviously from across the UK. Leeds has already introduced a system and Swansea is on the way.

One area where First believes that public transport can make a real difference to people's travel patterns and to the quality of life in city centres is through park-and-ride schemes. Buses can only ever provide a door-to-door service for a lucky minority whose journeys start and end right at a bus stop. Park-and-ride can do the next best thing. People can start their journeys by car and park them right by a shuttle service going straight to the shops and offices they need to reach. No bus will leave until the one behind has arrived and

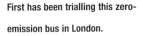

First has been trialling this zero-emission bus in London.

bus lanes will be used to leapfrog the morning commuters. The parking zone itself will be far enough from the city to avoid commuters getting tangled up in traffic on their way to it by car.

More than just a logo

By the time First expanded into North America in 1999, the company had been going for over ten years. It had accumulated bus and rail companies across the UK but each still had its own different livery and brand – sometimes more than one. Most of the ones First inherited were garish, primitive and un-appealing. They were certainly not likely to entice passengers out of their cars.

The man in the street did not have a clue who First was or that they were travelling on one of their vehicles. In truth it did not much matter to them who was providing the service. To them it was just the local bus or train company. Often that was what the local Managing Director wanted them to think – after all it was what he (and at that time it was always a he) believed. Their local companies were their own fiefdoms. Sometimes these managers resented interference from head office. They were traditional bus or rail men who had cut their teeth in the public sector. They believed they knew their markets, their fleet and their customers.

While there were design and style guidelines and supporting marketing

Four of the 197-strong Aberdeen bus fleet.

One of the new First rail liveries.

campaigns and materials, the focus had been on growing the company rather than doing what some bus managers would have considered tidying up at the margins. In any event, branding was expensive and the cost of reliverying buses would come out of their bottom line.

To some in the company that was the way it should stay, and to this day there are transport companies that still operate with a range of localised brands while the corporate identity is little known. There are some advantages. You can keep local brands and values and, in the event of local performance slipping, you are not polluting the brand. One major transport company was rumoured to be about to create a national brand a few years ago when a coach overturned and met the full glare of national publicity. The plan was quickly dropped into the 'too difficult' tray.

But First took the view that a national brand would help it drive up standards. Local companies would not be able to hide behind their local livery. Performance lapses would be seen as letting the group down too. It was not until a company managing directors' conference at the start of the new millennium that the company took the decision to adopt standard liveries for bus and rail fleets. For a company that was loath to waste hard-earned income on a corporate identity, corporate structure and branding, this represented that it was time for First to start to demonstrate the company's coming of age.

Even then it was agreed that there would be two bus liveries, not one. There would be a premium brand that would denote a service was being operated by brand-new vehicles and a not dissimilar livery that would differentiate it from the newer vehicles. This way the company believed it could highlight its massive investment in new vehicles. The premium livery was already in service in Aberdeen's new bus fleets and it was being rolled out to other companies as new vehicles arrived at their depots. Trains were to have a livery that, although it clearly came from the same stable, would be better able to withstand the operating conditions faced.

To satisfy both company accountants and media always critical of expenditure on branding it was planned to phase in the changes over three years as vehicles were due for heavy maintenance, when they were traditionally repainted or revinyled. For the first two years it was a branding nightmare in towns and cities across the UK. New vehicles would arrive in the brand-new livery – nicknamed 'Barbie' by company wits and the industry. Older vehicles due for a deep overhaul would emerge from their depots in the so-called 'Barbie 2' livery, while the remainder of the fleet cruised the streets in their pre-First garish colours.

In the UK's biggest bus market, London, the branding rules were completely different. Routes were tendered by Transport for London and, while winning bidders had to provide new fleets, they had to be branded in the traditional red colours of London buses.

Changing the livery on the railways was an even bigger brand challenge. Train sets often had to be broken up and put into different formations as an

Part of the quality fleet used on First's airport coach links.

An articulated bus in service in west London.

One of First Hull Trains' Pioneer Class 222 trains at King's Cross Station.

The yellow school bus brand is more than eighty years old and recognised across the world.

individual carriage's heavy maintenance fell due. It was in this maintenance period that coaches were automatically renewed. For many months trains were sometimes an unappealing mix of old and new liveries.

The changes were not just for the brand. They brought customer benefits too. Vehicle interiors were made more appealing with more subdued lighting, better seating and colour schemes, and every vehicle was promised regular deep cleaning outside and in.

In America branding opportunities were rather different. The company's yellow school bus fleet – even at the outset bigger than the company's entire UK bus operations – had to be painted the traditional school bus yellow, and normally the only branding allowed on the side of the vehicle was for the school bus district that was contracting the route.

The same was true for the mass transit services that First operated in major US cities. Almost invariably they were branded to the tendering authority's livery. The company's branding needed to be more subtle. Often the brand managers had to be content with a small First roundel and First Student sign discreetly placed on the vehicle.

Promotional materials and uniforms were a different matter, though. Tremendous thought went into choosing all First's livery, which was market tested with staff, managers and customers. Inside vehicles just as much care was taken with lighting, colour co-ordination and comfort. Everything was done to achieve designs of seating and colour to create a calm, soothing atmosphere.

But developing the pink and magenta Barbie livery was just the start. There had to be brand values to back it up. And developing a corporate brand and values meant that the local fiefdoms had to be challenged head on. No longer could they come up with their own local products, marketing advertising, liveries, fares initiatives, and so on.

To get buy-in from the local bus and rail managing directors, they were invited to join working groups set up to devise the new values and standards. Some entered the programme more enthusiastically than others, who hoped this new threat would fade quietly away as operational challenges got in the way – as had happened sometimes in the past. This time the faint hearts and Luddites were proved wrong. Different groups looked at issues such as recruitment and training, rewards and incentives for staff, service delivery, and so on.

For example on recruitment it was quickly agreed that it was pointless to reinvent the wheel every time a company needed to recruit bus drivers. Common templates for advertisements, recruitment and training styles were introduced and pay and benefits packages were designed to be appealing to new staff. It was common sense really and it meant less work and cost on recruiting and better-quality recruits.

And staff needed to become particularly important parts of the brand appeal. They were in the front line, meeting passengers daily, and needed to be ambassadors for the company. At one end of the scale they needed to look smart and tidy, and here First had to re-examine the whole issue of staff uniforms that staff had to buy into, that worked with the livery of the fleet and that would be popular with customers. Shona Byrne, the then marketing manager, remembers it all well. There were also good business reasons for having one generic uniform, she said. 'Twenty different uniforms, all local, made no sense. We could get better quality, better price and better conformity.'

The company went out to tender to different suppliers for what would be an initial contract of some £2.5 million. There were fashion parades for staff across the regions with models brought in to demonstrate the designs. The final choice had to be practical, tough, all weather, flexible and something that staff wanted to wear. Designs were produced in a mix-and-match fashion so everyone had a choice and did not have to look exactly the same.

Customers got a particular look-in on the interior design of vehicles and

The company goes to enormous lengths to make sure uniforms reflect the brand and are both popular and practical for the staff who have to wear them.

the seat styles. Two different buses were fitted out with different types of seating, livery and internal fittings, and sent to big towns so that customers could give First their views. Their thoughts were incorporated into future designs.

All this was just the start. As the company matured it started to develop premium brands for initiatives like guided busways, the Overground network and later the **ftr**. Driving these changes were attempts to make customers feel they were getting something special and different. Bob Tebb recalled in Leeds how he came under fire from a passenger who had seen one of her specially branded guided buses in use on another route. It was not on, she said.

Branding guidelines bored right down into what to the outsider might seem trivial things but to the industry are crucial. Take the humble bus timetable for example. Research showed that people found bus routes and timetables confusing and many had no concept that there was actually a service running close to them that could prove very useful.

If First was to get passengers back on to public transport, it had to put an end to that. Cue the Overground network. Started in Glasgow, each route and bus, the marketing materials, even the whole network, were branded so that they were recognisable and readily understandable. Soon it was rolled out across the UK and any First bus user could arrive in another corner of the country and recognise a familiar system.

And, as First hoped, staff became proud of the livery they wore, and of the fleet branding.

First's newest railway station – the interchange at St Pancras
International which links First Capital Connect passengers with
Eurostar, inter-city rail services and the London tube network.

Meeting challenges

Sense and sensitivity

There is a popular misconception among people in Britain that public transport has all been deregulated and privatised. In practice First and other public transport operators have to work in a regulatory and administrative minefield that raises the cost base, limits investment and restricts service improvements. Brakes are applied on the industry by a civil service and local government culture in which the simple and safe solution for bureaucrats is to say 'no' to everything. No one will be blamed for stopping an innovation, but saying 'yes' often means taking a difficult decision and having to be answerable for it later. It takes vision and leadership to break that mould.

There are rules for everything and they range from the sublime to the ridiculous. Many are utterly sensible and there to protect the health and safety of the public, promote healthy competition, ensure frequency and diversity of services and set rigorous standards for the construction of buses and trains.

Many rules are set in Brussels. In the rest of Europe there is a healthy pragmatism about the implementation of EU legislation. In the UK there is a long tradition of civil servants gold-plating them, overspecifying and complicating a perfectly simple proposal. Disabled toilets on trains are a case in point. Quite rightly there are regulations for their inclusion. Elsewhere in Europe disabled

First's freight operations help keep maintenance engineers supplied with ballast for track renewal.

On a rail network often operating at or near capacity, track maintenance can cause delays to passengers.

loos are efficient and effective. In the UK the design for each disabled loo includes corridor and seating space and is so prescribed and so space demanding that one can take the space of up to ten passenger seats.

As is so typical of a micro-managing civil service, officials must have looked at the problem without setting it in the context of the commercial operation of a railway service and the way all passengers use trains. Unfortunately administrators across the UK do not operate on the basis of 'How can we best facilitate an initiative in the best interests of the passenger or consumer?' Their work is so compartmentalised that at desk level each team is only looking at cost, price, safety, vehicle regulations or disabled access or whatever, completely losing sight of the big picture and what the consumer wants or the operator is trying to deliver.

First's passenger train companies operate on franchise contracts let by government. They only operate the trains – they have no control whatsoever over signals, track, infrastructure maintenance or investment. Even though they pay the infrastructure provider for the maintenance carried out on their lines, they have no say in when, how or if it will be carried out. They are completely at the mercy of the signalman employed by that infrastructure company about whether their passenger trains are given priority over a freight train.

In many cases now, train companies are operating free of subsidy and have to pay the government a premium for operating services. First Great Western must pay the government a total of £1 billion over ten years for the privilege of operating the services while First Capital Connect will pay the government £800 million for its nine-year franchise. Passengers' very legitimate grumbles about not enough seats or trains are often beyond the remit of a train operator to rectify. For example more trains are dependent on the network provider having a spare train path at peak times (unlikely) and the government being prepared to invest in new rolling stock that may not be part of its contract with the train company.

Today it is the government that dictates which rolling stock goes to what train operator, and whether they should have new trains – or even old ones. Train company operations are tightly specified by government and closely monitored. Failure to meet them can result in a franchise being taken away. They include performance, reliability, safety, investment, cleanliness, security, and so on. In some contracts even the amount of litter on the track at station platforms can entail fines for the train operator – even though the litter is dropped by passengers and can only be recovered by Network Rail staff.

Far from being a licence to print money, success depends crucially on being able to grow the number of passengers and to cut costs. And when there is

Just some of the vast number of documents that rail companies have to submit to the government in their bids to run rail franchises.

The new underground platforms for First Capital Connect at St Pancras International.

success the government have chosen to take a share of operators' profits, over and above the hefty premium they are already taking from them.

Nonetheless First has tried at different times to help advance the debate about the future of the railways in the UK, even commissioning and paying for a report to examine the feasibility of a TGV-style high-speed line from London to South Wales – only to be told by the government-owned Strategic Rail Authority (SRA), then being managed by a former railway business accountant, that they did the strategic thinking for the railways. Unfortunately Parliament did not agree. The Transport Select Committee's seventh report, in 2004, said: 'We found little evidence of the SRA leading the debate in the development of new thinking about the railway, or even engaging fully with many who are contributing to that debate.'

If there is one single piece of legislation that has had train and bus operators tearing their hair out since even before it was enacted, it is the Department of Trade and Industry sponsored 1998 Competition Act that came into force in 2000. It has set government department against government department and irritated the very public it was trying to protect.

As so often happens, the legislation was designed with the best of intentions, to prevent companies from engaging in anti-competitive behaviour through price-fixing and market domination, but its success depended on a pragmatic interpretation of the law and that didn't happen. To make matters worse, civil servants were given huge enforcement powers in pursuit of new victims. The government's own description of their powers shows that 'investigators are able to launch "dawn raids", and to enter premises with reasonable force'.

Transport companies warned the government what would happen as the draft legislation was going through Parliament, but it is only now, years later, that wrongs are being righted. To compound the problems, in the rest of Europe they take a more pragmatic view of legislative anomalies. Not in Britain, where the Office of Fair Trading (OFT), the competition policeman, has been known to rush up many blind alleys.

So what's the fuss about? As a starting point one could say that with about 90 per cent of UK journeys being by car it should go without saying that the vast majority of the competition buses and trains face is with private vehicles. And, if public transport is going to be effective and attract passengers back to it (which has long been government policy), then public transport operators need to make journeys as smooth, regular, simple and uncomplicated as they possibly can. That works best if services are at regular intervals throughout the day and fares are easily remembered so people can have the right change to hand. That is common sense, unless you are drawing up government legislation or implementing it as the OFT has sometimes done.

One case that used to be talked about in the industry apparently involved a couple of rural bus operators who decided that a rural route could only cope with two bus services (one from each operator) every hour. They decided that it would be better for the passenger if one bus company ran a vehicle on the hour and the other on the half hour, and that they charged the same fare. Not so according to the OFT. Those two bus companies colluded with each other to distort the market and fix prices. Regulations would have been met if one bus had been on the hour and one five minutes earlier to sweep up all the passengers. Passengers would have had to wait fifty-five minutes for the next bus and still not be sure what fare they would be charged, but the minutiae of the legislation would have been satisfied. With rural bus routes it is often simply a question of what operators can do to help them survive rather than a question of market distortion.

Rodney Dickinson, who until his retirement from First, worked tirelessly with national and local government to make sure buses were able to deliver for the passenger.

RIGHT: Edinburgh, where the OFT took two and a half years to find that First was not the dominant bus operator.

First was an occasional victim of the so-called 'dawn raids' that OFT civil servants got so excited about. In co-ordinated raids at different depots, a group of men would burst in and frighten the secretaries in managers' offices, searching and confiscating papers and computers. This happened to First several times. A classic example was in Edinburgh, where the local council-owned bus operation resented any competition from First and in September 2001 complained to the OFT that First was abusing its dominant position in the city. The OFT heavies were sent in. First was stunned by such a ploy since (as the OFT later confirmed) First only operated 20 per cent of the mileage in the city and had 20 per cent of the turnover. By contrast, the complainant operated 70 per cent of the mileage and had 70 per cent of the revenue.

Far from using its judgement and summarily kicking out the complaint, the OFT's enquiries lasted more than two-and-a-half years. It was only in April 2004 that an OFT press notice reported:

The OFT received a complaint from a rival bus operator, Lothian Buses plc, that First Edinburgh was abusing a dominant position by predatory pricing and by increasing services in the Greater Edinburgh area.
Lothian also alleged that First Edinburgh used profits from other routes to subsidise its routes within the Greater Edinburgh area.

The OFT has concluded that it was not abusive for First Edinburgh to reduce its fares or increase services as the balance of evidence suggests that this was a reasonable commercial strategy, from which passengers benefited, rather than an unlawful attempt to push Lothian out of the market.

The OFT investigation found that Lothian, rather than First Edinburgh, was the largest bus operator in the Greater Edinburgh area, but that First Edinburgh was likely to be dominant in the area surrounding Edinburgh. In some circumstances a firm that has a dominant position in one market may be found to have abused that position by conduct in another market.

The OFT found evidence that First Edinburgh's prices were low enough in comparison to its costs to raise questions about predation. However there was evidence that First Edinburgh did not intend to drive Lothian (the larger firm locally) from the market, and that it did not believe that it was capable of doing so. More compelling evidence was found that First Edinburgh was pricing low in an attempt to establish a more secure commercial basis for its Edinburgh operation.

The two-and-a-half years it took the OFT to see the blindingly obvious cost First hundreds of thousands of pounds and umpteen thousand hours of management time. The OFT reported proudly that along the way it had demanded a raft of documentation from the company down to individual route level. Much of that had to be specially prepared because it was not remotely necessary for running the business.

If only it had stopped there. Unfortunately the OFT decided to interfere in railway franchises too. Preparing each bid costs about £3 million and thousands of man hours before the OFT comes along and reports most of First's bids to the Competition Commission because it fears market domination. A classic case of the OFT at its most absurd was directed at First's bid for the East Coast Mainline rail franchise running between London King's Cross, north-east England and Scotland. First's bid was referred because the Aberdeen company also had local bus operations in Yorkshire. Another bidder was not referred even though, if it had won, it would have been operating every single daytime express train service between London and Scotland on both sides of the Pennines, thanks to its stake in Virgin Trains. It is difficult to understand the logic.

Time after time the OFT referred First bids for a railway franchise to the Competition Commission. That meant more hearings, more time wasting, more lawyers and a lot more cost. Fortunately the Commission is made of stern stuff and not one of the referrals resulted in any change of consequence. While this might sound like a small bit of bureaucratic merry-go-round, it had a very different impact on FirstGroup and its passengers. Every case took months, involved mountains of paperwork and took senior managers away from their day job of running train and bus services.

At the time these second-round franchises were being let, the process was being run by the government-owned SRA. At the start of privatisation a small organisation called the Office of Passenger Rail Franchises oversaw the break-up of British Rail's state-run passenger rail operations and the packaging of them into twenty-five passenger rail franchises. Once these franchises were out of the way, the new Labour government set up the SRA under the late Sir Alistair Morton, the much respected manager who had delivered the Channel Tunnel project.

Bus regulation

Since First owns outright the bus companies it operates in the UK, the bus sector presents First with far more opportunities to develop innovative new services and to invest in new fleets but, make no mistake, it is still a highly regulated business.

Lined up to control them are all these:

- **Treasury:** which sets the level of fuel duty rebate available for bus services – an important factor on marginal services. Aircraft and many trains face no fuel duty whatsoever. It is only the weakest members of society who have to pay it.
- **Department for Transport:** which polices the relationship between operators and the local authorities they serve and legislates for any structural change.
- **Traffic Commissioners:** who register bus services and police their performance.
- **Passenger Transport Executives:** which exist in major metropolitan areas to oversee and, where necessary, to commission rail and bus services they believe the community needs.

- **Transport for London:** which tenders all bus services in Greater London and dictates service volumes, performance standards and even vehicle age for the routes it is operating.
- **Vehicle and Operator Service Agency:** which ensures all vehicles are fit for purpose and legally compliant. They also enforce drivers' hours and licensing requirements.
- **Local authorities:** which let tenders for socially necessary but non-commercial services and have to provide the infrastructure which will allow bus services to perform effectively.
- **Office of Fair Trading:** which ensures that there is no collusion between operators to ensure co-ordinated services.
- **Competition Commission:** to make sure operators do not get too joined up and have too large a market share – irrespective of whether the services they provide are in the public interest.

These organisations all have an important role to play in helping to ensure that bus operators are held to account for the safe and efficient operation of their services, but let nobody think a bus company is answerable to no one.

On a day-to-day basis the most regular contact is with local authorities. Effective bus services depend crucially on a strong partnership between operator and local authority. Where it works well, it is brilliant – First invests in brand-new bus fleets for an entire city while the local authority provides the bus priority measures on key corridors.

When it does not work so well this relationship can be one of the biggest and most frustrating problems bus operators face. Across the country there are some real local-authority stars. They recognise that the only way to get their voters out of the car and back on to public transport is by a partnership of public transport operator and local authority, with the former providing the services and new fleets and the second the bus priority measures that will give public transport the edge on increasingly congested roads.

Across the UK there are many city-wide examples of the benefits that this co-operation can bring. A classic example is the city of York where First operates fleets of brand-new buses as well as park-and-ride schemes ringing the city – paying the council for the privilege. That is because the city has encouraged First by introducing radical bus priority lanes and gated areas in the heart of the city that are restricted for most other vehicles.

More priority measures such as these are urgently needed to separate buses from traffic.

Sadly, though, progress in most parts of the UK is painfully slow. Even where local authorities are ideologically supportive of boosting public transport use, they prefer to implement softer measures that do not bring about behavioural change. It is one thing to promote a voluntary car-free day, but quite another to take away a lane of traffic and give it over to a bus priority lane.

The government has provided many levers for local authorities to use but there are no penalties for not using them. They range from congestion charging to workplace parking levies, keeping parking penalty revenues and government-funding support for major schemes. Unfortunately it is hard for many authorities to reach a political consensus on what needs to be done, and when they do the proposals or their scale can be so watered down as to be ineffective.

The local-authority drivers of change with a track record of success involve introducing bus priority measures and park-and-ride schemes, restricting car parking, raising car parking prices, restricting city centre access to non-essential vehicles, and enforcing the measures and making them all widespread enough to make a difference. At the outset none of these measures will have anyone leaping for joy, and transport operators cannot demonstrate the benefits that will follow until they can fight their way through the traffic. Hence the reluctance of local authorities to rise to the challenge.

When a local authority has the courage to do that, local politicians may find their highways or public works department is not up to the task. Rather than crack on with a scheme on a trial basis and then consult on whether it is work-ing and worth keeping, officials will often enter a seemingly endless round of inconclusive consultation which postpones delivery for another day. One First manager recalled a company presentation to local councillors. They were ex-tremely enthusiastic about the initiative, which required little action on their officers' part – merely to create a safe stopping point near a school. Their highway engineer dampened their enthusiasm by saying that he would be in a position to begin his minor part of the initiative the year after next. For an industry and a company that wants to press ahead with a scheme these delays can be deeply frustrating.

One plus point, though. First now has a much more constructive relation-ship with both the OFT and the Competition Commission than the turbulent times described earlier might indicate. Maybe there is a growing recognition that transport operators are not the bogeymen the civil servants once thought they were, and are genuinely trying to deliver customer service to their cus-tomers. Maybe the ground rules have changed, and perhaps they have found some more deserving targets.

Growing green

First is committed to reducing its impact on the environment. By 2020 First UK Bus aims to reduce its carbon emissions by 25% – an ambitious target.

Since the start of the new millennium it has become fashionable for companies to demonstrate their green credentials – sometimes thanks to prompts from governments, environmentalists and ethical investors.

First is one of that rare breed of companies that recognised its responsibili-ties and opportunities from the early days of GRT. Delivering train and bus services is, in itself, a green industry since the passengers the fleet carries are taking thousands of polluting cars off the road and reducing transport's emissions – UK bus operations alone save 200,000 tonnes of carbon dioxide emissions a year that cars would otherwise emit.

But that was just the starting point for First. It had been keen on cleaner fuels from the early days of the company and by 1999 it had committed to running its entire UK bus fleet on ultra low-sulphur diesel, cutting 3,500 tonnes of carbon monoxide and 300 tonnes of sulphur from bus operations every year. Since then it has started using the new 5 per cent bio diesels.

On rail too the company was looking at how to cut emissions from the diesel

Politicians like Labour's Neil Kinnock
(now Lord Kinnock) backed First's use
of greener fuel.

fleet. It worked with manufacturers to produce a new engine for their high-speed train diesel fleet to see how much more could be achieved. The test trains showed that some emissions could be halved and, as a result, they were introduced across the fleet.

The company has always looked at alternative and greener power supplies for its vehicles – ranging from a look at electrifying a new high-speed line from London to South Wales through to an interest in the technology to run trains by magnetic levitation, as the Chinese have achieved on the route from Shanghai Airport into the city.

For the future the company is looking at hydrogen developments – it has already been taking part in UK pilots of hydrogen-powered vehicles. It has also been looking at hybrid vehicles which can run on battery power when operating in city centres. First is simultaneously working with bus manufacturers Wrights in Northern Ireland to identify how the weight of new vehicles can be reduced and fuel consumption improved. And even at the drawing-board stage of the new **ftr** streetcar initiative the two companies were talking about hybrid power and alternative fuels for later generations of the vehicle. As a result of all its efforts the company scores well in Business in the Community Social Responsibility Index.

A greener way to travel. First is looking
with interest at the magnetic levitation
system run by the Chinese on their
route from Shanghai city to the airport.

With his engineering background, Lockhead is only too happy to take a look in the engine compartment.

First Capital Connect was the first UK rail company to achieve ISO 14001 accreditation.

An example of the commitment First has put into being environmentally friendly is the way operating companies have been working towards ISO 14001 accreditation, the recognised international standard for monitoring and managing the company's impact on the environment. Today more than half of the company's UK operations have achieved the standard, which provides a systematic approach to cutting waste and increasing recycling. In 2008 First Capital Connect became the first UK rail company to achieve the standard.

For many years the company has sponsored environmental awards within the group for both individuals and operating companies, and it has been impressive to see the benefits that have been achieved through some of the work.

Back in 2005 the company approved its own climate-change policy, which was reinforced in 2007 when the company also introduced its very own Climate Change Strategy focusing on carbon dioxide emissions but including a much broader programme covering atmospheric emissions, energy, resource use, waste disposal and biodiversity. The company has set a target of a 20 per cent reduction in emissions in the Rail division and 25 per cent in the UK Bus division by 2020.

An artist's impression of part of the company headquarters in Aberdeen.

The new group headquarters in Aberdeen is leading the way, with plans for using renewable energy and recycling water from the bus washes. To keep to its delivery programme, the company is held to account in its annual corporate social responsibility report to investors.

Meanwhile, the company's commitment to greenness has been recognised in a range of national awards.

Public perceptions

The difference between reality and perception about public transport in the UK illustrates the problems First has to battle with in winning passengers back off the roads. People who actually use public transport consistently have a much higher opinion of it than those that don't.

A 2007 government omnibus survey recorded that 72 per cent of bus users felt their local services were good or very good and just 13 per cent thought they were poor. However, only 58 per cent of non-users felt services in their area were good while 21 per cent felt they were poor. A similar government survey on rail travel in 2006 showed that 70 per cent of users rated services as good while only 56 per cent of non-users felt the same way.

A French TGV power car arrives in Paris from Zurich. These trains do 186 mph compared with a maximum of 125 mph for UK domestic rail services.

First's platform staff are always available when help is required.

While statisticians might quarrel with interpretations of the findings, an obvious one would be that the political and media comment on public transport distorts attitudes to it. Regular users are less swayed by the torrent of criticism of services because, as customers, they know better. When newspapers report surveys showing that 20 per cent of passengers are unhappy with their journeys, their readers are statistically likely to be among the 80 per cent who are happy but don't get mentioned.

First and other operators can only look longingly across the Channel at European pride in their flagship transport projects – take for example the French and their high-speed TGV rail network. There is an acceptance of higher taxes to pay to develop world-class systems like these. However, although the UK has no state-funded flagship projects and little of the public-sector investment that much of the rest of Europe has benefited from, UK private operators have gone a long way to revolutionise investment in the non-infrastructure aspects of transport where they do have a responsibility. Sadly there has been little recognition for it from politicians, public and the media – particularly when their investments have had to run on overcrowded roads and a fragile rail infrastructure over which they have no control.

Billions of pounds of private-sector money have poured in to renew rail and bus fleets since privatisation, increasing the availability of public transport and sending the average age of fleets down to new record lows. New technology

Every day 9 million people travel on a First bus or train.

has been introduced to make services safer and more reliable. Massive amounts of time and money have been devoted to making journeys more comfortable and as near door-to-door as possible.

But First and other public transport operators live and operate in a land where the car is king and, while little is heard of public transport improvements, much is made of any late train or bus. National and local newspapers have their motoring supplements and the travel pages are full of aviation deals to all corners of the world. Television channels have endless programmes devoted to car and plane travel. In that world there is little space to record the regularly delayed flights or the unpredictability of road travel, or to contrast door-to-door times or costs with public transport.

The public is long overdue some explanations and analysis on why we don't, as a nation, have a strategic approach to transport or the grand projects to deliver it. Until the public has a clear idea of the underinvestment and what could be achieved on their behalf, they will put up with the traffic congestion and overcrowded railway lines that have become the accepted norm. If the media cannot provide this service there will be no pressure for change and our nation will remain in the shadow of our European neighbours.

Meanwhile perception is everything, but it has to be set in the context of reality. Of course operators must be hounded for repeated poor service, but let's put it in that context.

Crowded trains will remain the reality until increased government funding becomes available.

Winning respect in the City

When Aberdeen's GRT floated on the stock market in 1994 it proved popular with investors. This was still the era of privatisations and the markets knew that the old public-sector operations were riddled with public-sector inefficiencies, high staffing levels and costs. When these were stripped out, the leaner, fitter businesses that emerged would have real potential for growth.

But, at the end of the day, in City eyes this was not a giant like British Telecom or British Gas, but just another local bus operator that had come to the market. Nevertheless, bus companies were popular with investors who searched out cash-generating businesses with highly visible earnings, and here was a good example. And the money that flotations raised created the war chests that allowed acquisitions to accelerate and bring even greater returns for shareholders.

Two of the eight buses used to support
First's national charity partnership with
Save the Children.

The flotation itself was a time of drama for the company as, almost on the eve of the market listing, Barry Stubbings, the leading adviser on the flotation, was murdered in London. Nonetheless, a shaken management team continued and on 5 May 1994 – when dealing started – GRT shares made a strong showing, rising from 161p to close their first day's trading at 171p with almost three million shares changing hands.

However, it was not until the company grew and diversified that the City really sat up and began to take notice. Early targets were the UK rail businesses, followed soon after by the first US acquisitions. Rail was a different type of business – it was a heavily regulated market, and therefore in City eyes a risky business. It also had a heavy cost structure and old working practices, but First soon proved it was able to bring its entrepreneurial flair to bear.

The first rail win was the First Great Eastern line, operating commuter services out to Essex and Suffolk; then came the acquisition of the already privatised Great Western Holdings with its inter-city services. Contracts came and went but by 2005 the company had built up the largest and most diversified rail portfolio in the UK and was the only company to offer sleeper, inter-city, commuter, regional and freight services.

Shareholders soon saw the benefits of First's US acquisition and the creation of an additional arm to its operations with an extra earnings stream. Much of the acquisition was financed by a rights issue, shareholders being given the opportunity to purchase more shares that the company generated for the event. At last they could see First had become a reliable long-term player which had identified a massive new market and had the security of five-year contracts with school boards. Investors liked the fact that First was a business that could ride out recessions. With bus services, if travel patterns dropped operators could always change the frequency of services to match the changing demand.

First Great Eastern train.

A First ScotRail train pulls out of
Waverley Station with the famous
Balmoral Hotel reflected in the window.

First GBRf locomotive.

That used to be a flexibility not open to the early railway franchises, where operators were contracted to run a fixed number of trains whether or not there were passengers on board. This changed with the second generation of rail franchises, with both government and operators sharing the risk – and the reward. In North America children still need to go to school, recession or not, and federal contracts still need to be serviced.

But if shareholders loved some of First's earlier acquisitions, they could really get excited over the acquisition of the giant Laidlaw yellow school bus company. The benefits just kept on coming. At first came the removal of Laidlaw from the US stock market listings with the $35 million annual compliance costs that the recent tough US corporate governance legislation had inflicted on US listed companies. Then there were the synergy savings of $150 million – that will flow through every year from 2008/9 onwards, from headquarters savings, removing duplicated posts and functions, and taking the best from each company.

And these savings could be rolled out across North America – school bus depots could be merged and brand-new purpose-built maintenance depots constructed on one site, allowing the other to be sold off. There would be extra benefits from reduced costs for fuel, procurement and insurance that the magnitudes of scale could deliver.

Out on the ground, school boards would feel the difference in terms of the benefits they could receive by outsourcing their school bus operations. Historically First Student (pre-Laidlaw) was able to offer school bus contracts that were up to 20 per cent cheaper than those provided in-house. With the combined efficiencies of Laidlaw and First Student those savings could potentially reach an amazing 40 per cent in some circumstances.

Also, even where school boards had ideological concerns about outsourcing, there is extra scope for business: First could procure their fleets, allowing them to take advantage of the huge discounts that a company ordering 5,000 buses a year can squeeze from the manufacturer. And hard-pressed school superintendents who can spend up to 30 per cent of their afternoons dealing with mothers who have failed to connect with their children at the right place or time could soon be able to free themselves of that burden, thanks to sophisticated computer barcode-type software being developed by First Student.

Entering the FTSE 100 Index of the UK's largest companies in December 2007 meant the company now had broader investor appeal, reaching out to tracker funds which invest across the Index. And that included major European and international investors who suddenly wanted to get to know more about the company. Across the City the announcement was acknowledged as a big achievement for a company just twenty years old. It was never a First objective but more a recognition of the company's size and scale.

Over the years First has steadily outperformed the FTSE Index and its shares have risen from a closing first-day price of 173p back in 1994 to peaks of over £8 in 2007. Along the way share prices have been buffeted by two Gulf wars, terror attacks, rocketing fuel prices, recessions, a credit crunch and a dotcom boom that encouraged shareholders to desert traditional sectors like transport for the make-believe land of internet start-up companies with no trading record and no profits.

When First entered the FTSE 100 in 2007 it was the only surface transport operator there, and it has been fascinating to watch the City's interest in the company change. Twice a year, at the time of the company's interim and full-year results, some fifty transport analysts are briefed on the company's performance during the reporting period.

Once the company had burst into the rail and North American markets, questioning after the presentations was often intense and sceptical. As the years passed and First grew and developed into its chosen markets, attitudes changed. First had done what it had said it was going to do and the tone of comments

First is now believed to be regarded by the City as the best-managed transport operator.

seemed to reflect that. Questioning seemed to be much more a question of understanding how something was being achieved rather than whether.

Lockhead attributes much of First's success in the City to a key female manager on the First team: Rachael Borthwick, the company's corporate communications director. Her infectious enthusiasm, gritty determination, warm personality and razor-sharp wit have inspired both company directors and her City audiences.

Another factor has been the way that, early on, the company quickly embraced the corporate social responsibility concept before it became increasingly relevant to investors and City ethical funds.

Meanwhile guiding City relations has been company Chairman Martin Gilbert, who believes that the City now regards First as the best-managed transport operator.

From strength to strength – First today and tomorrow

A casual observer of the world of public transport might suggest that First's rapid rise was simply a matter of being in the right place at the right time. There's no doubt that getting in on the ground at bus deregulation and rail franchising in the UK helped, but it in no measure explains how First carved such a huge niche for itself so quickly and in such a volatile area.

Passengers always look forward to this part of the Devon coastline on their journey to London.

There were already big beasts roaming in the jungle way before GRT was privatised. The shelf life of a new local authority buyout was not a long one. New owners either struggled in a more competitive world or decided to cash in their gains and sell out to a bigger operator. The switch from public transport use to cars was spreading, making traffic congestion progressively worse and operating conditions more challenging. Then, just as the deregulated bus market started to stabilise, both a recession and the first Gulf War came along, sending fuel prices through the roof and reducing the number of journeys people were making.

When rail privatisation was implemented in the mid 1990s it was seen as the last fling of a dying Tory government, bringing with it all the uncertainties of

The workhorses of the rail freight fleet.

what an incoming Labour government would do with it. But soon after Labour signalled that it would not reverse the changes, we had the second Gulf War and Railtrack, the private-sector rail infrastructure provider, imploded. The entire railway industry went into paralysis for over a year as concerns about infrastructure safety placed draconian speed restrictions on the network. Oil prices went through the roof again.

As if this wasn't enough, the world's stock markets decided in their wisdom that internet start-up companies with no trading records, no profits and no credible business plan were the shape of the future. Money poured out of traditional stocks in the rush for fool's gold, limiting investment and growth opportunities for companies that were already delivering profits and had been for years. And as oil soared to well over $130 a barrel in 2008, the world's banks pulled the rug from under the credit market as they rushed to slam the stable door on their subprime failings. Throughout, First was not deflected from its expansion programme.

While all this was going on First was busy expanding into the North American markets it had first entered in 1999. By 2007 it was accounting for nearly half of turnover – despite the fact that the continent was regarded by the City as the graveyard of British businesses.

Suddenly the successes of FirstGroup did not look as if they could be put down to luck, chance or being in the right place at the right time. So what were the reasons for the company's success? It stuck rigidly to the businesses it knew well: running bus and rail companies and maintenance operations.

It never paid over the odds for companies it acquired, walking away from the table and letting a rival squander its shareholders' money if the price got too high for First's business model. It brought efficiency to the operations it had and searched for organic growth by stretching and expanding its businesses.

First recognised that investing in the business and focusing on safety, customer service, reliability, frequency and affordable fares would pay dividends in terms of passenger growth. It saw that economies of scale in purchasing would bring greater savings and make the company's operations more competitive in bidding rounds.

It saw that standardisation of service quality, maintenance, marketing, brand, purchase, quality, finance systems, human resources, recruiting, pensions and training would boost performance and lower the cost base.

The company operates in a sector that is as recession proof as it is possible to get. Even while oil price rises are hurting (a major cost factor for the company), it is bringing in more passengers and more revenue. As Lockhead reported at the half year results in 2007, just as oil prices were spiking at nearly $100 a barrel: 'We have seen signs of a modal shift in a way we have not seen before, and it is driven by pump prices as much as it is by congestion.'

Public transport is coming back into its own and that can only be good news for a company like First. Oil supply has peaked, there is no more room on the UK roads for cars; and that forces governments and local authorities to look seriously at managing road space, giving more priority to public transport and encouraging drivers and their passengers to use public transport. And, across the countries where First operates, if subprime shocks and recessions lead to business collapses, children still need to get to school and people still need to get

An artist's impression of the new Aberdeen headquarters.

about, and that means a busy time for public transport. Historically season-ticket sales suffer but a second car gives way to public transport journeys as families tighten their belts.

First's chairman Martin Gilbert with Sir Moir Lockhead at the wheel.

As if that was not enough of a safeguard for First, there is another. More than half of the company's business is with the public sector and contracted for periods of up to ten years. And many of those contracts, particularly in the railway industry, have what is known as cap-and-collar agreements which introduce profit sharing after a fixed level of profits is made – but also limit the losses that First can take in the event of a downturn.

These business fundamentals have stood the test of time and taken the company to where it is today – the largest private-sector public transport operator in the world. The company carries more than nine million passengers a day right across North America and the United Kingdom. It runs 82,500 buses and coaches and 2,000 railway carriages, and employs 137,000 people from both sides of the Atlantic to the Pacific Ocean, from Alaska to Mexico and from the northern tip of Scotland down to Germany.

It is a vast empire running twenty-four hours a day, taking children to school and back and commuters to work and home, keeping police forces on the streets and parts of the US military running, providing the disabled with transport and opening up the US with the Greyhound bus network.

So what does the future hold for First? If it is to stick to its core strategy, it

has now nearly reached maturity in UK markets and will have to look to new markets overseas in the main. Growth in the UK will come from growing passenger numbers rather than significant acquisitions in the bus market or many new rail franchises. European countries are now being forced by Brussels to liberalise their own transport markets, although they are carefully skewing the competition to favour their own national businesses.

First has, in the past, forged alliances with French, Danish and Dutch rail operators to understand European businesses better. It has acquired its first European operations with a network of German bus businesses and a coach/air link in Dublin, and it has investigated opportunities from eastern Europe to the Atlantic and the Mediterranean.

But the company has not turned its eyes away from the rapidly expanding economies in India, China, the rest of South East Asia and South America if the opportunities look like another one-way bet.

What can be certain is First's determination to bend new technology to transport applications. The company was one of the pioneers in using more environmentally friendly diesel, in using hydrogen-powered buses and in looking at hybrid power supplies for part of its fleet. It has even explored the use of Maglev-type magnetic-powered trains with Lockhead testing for himself the link from Shanghai to the city's airport. The motives for doing so are many – it does actually care about the environment, the cost of diesel is going through the roof, it may be able to partner with the public sector in using greener (but more expensive) technologies and it is researching its own initiatives for greening the fleet.

Meanwhile Lockhead believes that there are real opportunities for greening the power supplies for the rail fleet with the electrification of additional lines using renewable energy or nuclear power to feed the trains. It is not beyond the bounds of possibility that fifty years after they were done away with, modern electric-powered trolley buses could come back into service.

Vehicle design is another challenge for the future. New buses may be more comfortable and more environmentally friendly, but the price for that is heavier vehicles and a worsening fuel consumption. First has partnered with Wrights, the Northern Ireland bus and coach builders, to try and build a better, lighter and more fuel-efficient bus. The old Routemasters, so popular with passengers, were also fuel efficient. A current double-decker weighs half as much again as a Routemaster and, as a result, only does five miles to the gallon – half the Routemaster figure.

Sir Moir Lockhead and Scotland's First Minister, Alex Salmond, in front of the foundation stone for the new company headquarters in Aberdeen.

RIGHT: A First Great Western high-speed train.

For the future, First is also keen to see a radical rethink of the shape of the next-generation railway passenger franchises. The artificial division between the company running the trains and the company running the signals and track maintenance is a recipe for delay and inefficiency. It certainly is not in the passenger's best interest and flies in the face of both experience and history. Neither the original railway companies nor old British Rail could have conceived such a divisive system.

First has explored and tried to promote the prospect of reintegration on the railways – with track, signals and trains all operated (but not owned) by the same company. In particular the company has suggested that the initiative be trialled in Scotland or the south west of England since any trial would work best where there was only one dominant train company, preventing cries of foul play by other operators.

The advantages are clear. Maintenance would be better co-ordinated to meet the needs of customers and services rather than the convenience of the infra-structure provider. With track, trains and signals all controlled by the same managers the spirit of co-ordination and co-operation would be much closer and the operator would have much better control over performance. Timetable planning would improve and signallers would be motivated – and managed – to make sure that trains were routed in the most effective way for passengers. No more freight trains being signalled in front of an inter-city service. Ownership of track would continue in government hands as today.

It is reassuring that, despite the lack of any clear national vision for transport or any flagship project that could make up a component part of one, First will be continuing with its own strategic research into climate-change implications, new technology, new markets and changing customer expectations – all backed by their long-standing commitment to investment in new fleet and infrastructure and quest for partnerships with the public sector.

If the company continues as today, it will relentlessly search for growth and, in its pursuit, actively seek to be both biggest and best at what it does. It is a matter of pride to a company that has come a long way very quickly.

A history of Aberdeen transport and the development of FirstGroup

Year	Activity
1833	The first Aberdeen regular bus service to run on a fixed timetable route operated with experimental steam bus. Ended when boiler exploded.
1850	Two new services introduced – horse-drawn buses: Royal Hotel to Stoneywood, fare 6d; new railway station to King Street, fare 3d.
1862	William Bain formed a private company to deliver a more lasting network of buses in Aberdeen.
1874	Aberdeen horse trams introduced, eventually supplanting other operations.
1898	Aberdeen Corporation bought horse tramways and extended route network.
1900	The first – but short-lived – motor-bus service introduced in Aberdeen.
1915	The first Aberdeen female 'conductorettes' employed.
1917	First Aberdeen female drivers.
1955	Aberdeen Transport Department abandoned trams and started bus-only operations.
1975	As a result of local government reorganisation Aberdeen Corporation Transport became Grampian Regional Transport.
1985	Moir Lockhead, formerly Chief Engineer at Strathclyde Buses in Glasgow, took his first management job as Director of Public Transportation at Grampian.
1985	The newly enacted Transport Act, designed to create a competitive market in public transport, came into force.
1986	Grampian Regional Transport registered as a stand-alone company and took over operations on Deregulation Day – 26 October.
1987	Grampian introduced more routes, new coaches for expanding tours and private hire operation and new ticketing initiatives for the 35 million passengers a year.
1987	Grampian bought the Aberdeen coach business of G E Mair Hire Services Ltd with its 20-strong fleet.
1988	Moir Lockhead and the management team approached the Regional Council with a proposal to purchase the company through a management/employee buyout. It would be owned as follows: 51% management, 33% employees, 16% financial institutions.
1989, 20 January	The newly formed GRT Holdings plc bought Grampian Regional Transport Ltd for £5.5 million and became the first local-authority bus fleet in private hands.
1989	Acquired Kirkpatrick of Deeside, the Banchory-based bus and coach operator.
1990	GRT's £8.5 million bid for Midland Scottish was accepted and the new company had its first acquisition, which had depots in Alloa, Balfron, Bannockburn, Larbert, Linlithgow and Oban.

Year	Activity
1993	Bid for Northampton Transport, which had a turnover of £4.3 million and pre-tax profit of £888,000, accepted.
1993, November	GRT's £7.4 million bid for Leicester City Bus Ltd and Leicester Country Bus Ltd accepted.
1994, April	Flotation of GRT, valuing the company at £57 million. Hundreds of employee shareholders who took up around 10% of the placing each made anything between £1,000 and £100,000.
1994, June	GRT acquired the Eastern Counties Bus Group for £6.7 million. For the previous six years the company had been run by a management buyout team who had bought the business from the National Bus Company. It operated local bus services across Norfolk and Suffolk.
1994, September	GRT put in an offer for SMT, which operated bus services in Edinburgh and the Lothians. GRT offered £10 million in cash and shares.
1994	GRT offered £2.17 million for Reiver Ventures Ltd, trading as Lowland Scottish in the Borders.
1995	UK's first guided busway opens in Ipswich.
1995	Leeds guided busway opens.
1995, June	GRT merged with Badgerline and the combined company became known as FirstBus.Together they became the second largest UK bus company. Badger brought with it: Bristol Omnibus Badgerline Buses Eastern National PMT Midland Red West Wessex of Bristol South Wales Transport Western National Thamesway Wessex National Rider Group Quickstep Travel.
1996	The newly merged GRT and Badgerline had a 24.5% stake in Great Western Holdings, the management buyout company which won the Great Western franchise, one of the three first privatised railway operators.
1996, March	FirstBus bought GMBN, the Greater Manchester Northern bus operator, which was valued at £47 million.
1996, June	The £110 million purchase of S B Holdings, operators of Strathclyde Buses, which made FirstBus the largest bus operator in the UK. The company ran two thirds of the buses in and around Glasgow.
1996, November	FirstBus won its first rail franchise outright – the Great Eastern Railway, the commuter railway service linking Essex with the City of London.
1997	Acquisition of Southampton CityBus with its operations across the Southampton and Portsmouth areas.
1997, February	FirstBus paid £54 million to buy its first London bus business, CentreWest, whose operations included those of the Berks Bucks Bus Company and their stake in Croydon Tramlink, which was to run the first London trams in nearly 50 years.
1997, November	First became the preferred purchaser of a 51% stake in the airport operated by Bristol City Council.

Year	Activity
1997, December	FirstBus changed its name to FirstGroup in recognition of the fact that the company was now broadening its public transport interests.
1998	Great Western Holdings, operators of Great Western trains, acquired by the company for £104.8 million, doubling its size.
1998, April	First took a 26% stake in New World First Holdings to run 88 bus routes criss-crossing Hong Kong.
1998, July	First bought London's largest independent bus operator, Capital City Bus of Dagenham, for £11.1 million.
1998	£30 million acquisition of South Yorkshire Mainline bus company.
1999	First enter USA market with purchase of Bruce Transportation for $36 million.
1999	First bought Ryder Public Transportation Services, catapulting the company to second largest operator of yellow school buses in North America. The purchase brought with it two new First businesses: First Transit, running city buses in the US, and First Services, maintaining public-sector transport fleets.
1999	Introduction of Glasgow Overground bus network, soon to be rolled out across the UK.
1999	Ladbroke Grove accident which killed 31 people.
1999	First committed itself to running its entire UK bus fleet on ultra low-sulphur diesel, cutting 3,500 tonnes of carbon monoxide and 300 tonnes of sulphur from bus operations every year.
2000	Partnered with BP to launch the Schools Charter, teaching children the importance of protecting the environment.
2000	First introduced a total safety audit for all its operations and brought in a zero tolerance culture for accidents and safety issues in the workplace.
2000	First extended its yellow bus operations to Canada, buying the Hertz Bus Company, Canada's third largest, with 735 vehicles.
2000, May	First started operating London's first trams for 50 years with the introduction of the new Croydon Tramlink services.
2000	Opening of new Bristol International Airport terminal, more than doubling airport's capacity.
2000	First ended its Far East operations with the sale of its 26% stake in New World First Holdings, operator of Hong Kong buses, making a profit of £14 million in 18 months on its original £24 million investment.
2001, January	First completed the sale of its 51% stake in Bristol International Airport to Macquarie Bank Limited and a Spanish company.
2001, June	First announced orders for the first 20 US-style yellow school buses for the commercial UK market.
2001	Bradford guided busway and second Leeds guided busway opened.
2002, January	First commercial US-style yellow school bus operations for the UK begin in Yorkshire.
2002	First started operating UK's first city-wide park-and-ride operation in York.

Year	Activity
2002, Summer	First delivered Manchester Commonwealth Games transport operations for athletes, officials and media with a fleet of 75 brand-new single-deck buses.
2002	FirstInfo, the fast-growing Plymouth-based call centre business, reached the milestone of handling 11 million calls a year through its 500 staff.
2002	US yellow bus growth through purchases of small companies and contract wins took yellow bus total to 15,500 – a 50% increase in three years.
2002	First part of UK first pilot scheme to deliver real-time bus information, allowing mobile phone users to ring their bus stop and find out when the next bus would arrive. Leicester pilot called StarText.
2003	First started trialling hydrogen-powered buses in London (in partnership with TfL and EU) which produce just fresh air and water, as part of an EU trial.
2003	First introduced its first combined joint railway control centre with Network Rail to ensure network is delivering to maximum efficiency for the passenger.
2003, May	First bought Coach USA's transit division, a wholly owned subsidiary of Stagecoach Group plc, for US$ 22.5 million. The business operates buses on behalf of transit authorities in states such as California, Florida and New York.
2003, August	First bought GB Railways, operators of Anglia Rail franchise, GB Rail and its rail-freightoperations and the open-access Hull Trains services.
2003, August	First won TransPennine Express franchise.
2003, November	First named as preferred bidder to run Thames Trains franchise for two years in run-up to award of Greater Western franchise.
2004, June	First won ScotRail franchise.
2005, December	First won Greater Western rail franchise.
2005, December	First won Thameslink Great Northern franchise and renamed it First Capital Connect.
2007, February	First announced proposed acquisition of Laidlaw, the largest operator of yellow school buses in North America and the operator of Greyhound buses.
2007	First entered continental Europe with the purchase of three family German bus companies in Mannheim, Ludwigshafen and Heidelberg.
2007, May	Launch of First's Climate Change Strategy.
2007, June	First bought Chester City Transport and its bus operations.
2007, September	Inaugural First Monster Challenge, a 120 km duathlon around the shores of Loch Ness to raise money for First's partnership with Save the Children.
2008	First ScotRail franchise extended to 2014.
2008	Yellow School Bus Commission reported.
2009	First's new global headquarters opens in Aberdeen.

INDEX

Entries in **bold** relate to illustrations and captions.

1986
Grampian Regional Transport
registered as a stand-alone company

1990
GRT successfully bids
£8.5 million for Midland Scottish

1995
GMT merges with
Badgerline to form
FirstBus

1997
FirstBus buys
CentreWest, its
first London bus
business

FirstBus renamed
FirstGroup to
reflect its
broadening public
transport interests

● Bus milestones

● Rail milestones

○ North American milestones

○ Corporate milestones

1989
Grampian Regional Transport
Holdings plc buys Grampian
Regional Transport Ltd to
become the first Scottish local
authority bus fleet in private
hands

1994
GRT floated on the
stock market with a
value of £57 million

1996
FirstBus buys GMBN, the
greater Manchester bus
operator.

Strathclyde Buses bought
for £110 million.

FirstBus wins the Great
Eastern rail franchise